Immortal Combat

Fr. Dwight Longenecker

Immortal Combat

Confronting the Heart of Darkness

SOPHIA INSTITUTE PRESS
Manchester, New Hampshire

Sophia Institute Press
Box 5284, Manchester, NH 03108
1-800-888-9344

www.SophiaInstitute.com

Sophia Institute Press® is a registered trademark of Sophia Institute.

ISBN 978-1-64413-290-6
eBook ISBN 978-1-64413-291-3

Library of Congress Control Number: 2020932960

You know the time; it is the hour now for you to awake from sleep. For our salvation is nearer now than when we first believed; the night is advanced, the day is at hand. Let us then throw off the works of darkness [and] put on the armor of light; let us conduct ourselves properly as in the day, not in orgies and drunkenness, not in promiscuity and licentiousness, not in rivalry and jealousy. But put on the Lord Jesus Christ, and make no provision for the desires of the flesh.

—Rom. 13:11–14

Contents

Foreword

You have in your hands a very good book, a very much *needed* book in an era in which the Church has largely lost sight of a major mission: direct confrontation with the devil. Is this not what Jesus was about? Did He not say He had come "to destroy the works of the devil" (1 John 3:8)? Wasn't it Christ who said He would recognize His followers — would know them! — by several standards, the first of which was casting out devils (Mark 16:17)?

Other questions rise from those. Do we emulate Jesus? Does the modern Church? Do those at the helm of Catholicism roam the hinterlands, commanding demons to leave the afflicted, as Jesus and His apostles did?

The answer, all too often, of course, is no: too often, at Mass, the reading of the day concerns demonic manifestations, but the subsequent homily doesn't mention them. There is little or no instruction in this regard. We rely instead on movies. In our hyperscientific, academic age, spiritual warfare has become *subjectum non gratum*. There are more canon lawyers — substantially more — than there are exorcists.

This is where Father Dwight Longenecker enters the picture — and the pulpit. Bold, imaginative, insightful, and engaging,

Immortal Combat

Father Longenecker forges ahead without fear or favor in naming where evil is, what it looks like, how it hides itself, and where it manifests itself the most (in society and in all of us). Most important in the eyes of this learned, intellectual, and practical priest, is how to expunge evil and stop it from returning.

And so it is that Father Longenecker ably tackles our culture of idolatry. He drills deep into this time of prevarication. Citing the mirages, exaggerations, and blatant untruths of our time, he shows how "people of the lie" have caused distress in every corner—and among those (don't be fooled!) of every politico-cultural stripe.

In so doing, this good priest agilely—critically—argues for a mystical, imaginative approach in addition to intellectuality. He shows how religiosity can cloak darkness—how it can portray itself as an angel of light. He graphically shows us the importance of forgiveness. He demonstrates the significance of simplicity and humility (really, the same thing) in keeping evil at bay, which is important when we remember that, as one psychologist put it, evil is the word "live" spelled backward.

Evil is also *living* backward, for darkness aims us at the inverse of good, in the direction of the nether regions.

Most importantly, we find *ourselves* in these pages.

Do you have resentment? Anger? Jealousy? Hidden pride? We are faced in this book with all we need to expiate, recognizing how the demon leads us first into depression or regression, then into oppression and obsession, and, finally into possession. Can you not in these words hear the *hiss* of the snake?

We live in a time when the devil is especially active (one might say "viral"), and thus at a time when a book like this by a solid, conversant priest—one who has been "around the horn"—is desperately needed. The necessity is to show the interaction between humans and nefarious components of the spiritual world, and how to handle and, in some cases, survive it. In a phrase, this book presents a Catholic framework for spiritual warfare, with vivid images of everything from minotaurs and Gorgons to dragons—which, as the reader will see, are not always the simple wanderings of fiction.

Father Longenecker does here what every priest should: he speaks about the devil and how he and his minions operate in our time.

According to reliable scholarship, Pope Leo XIII (1810–1903) had a vision of the effects Satan would have after the pope's death. It foretold a horrible trial for the Church.

Do we not see this around us? And by eliminating mystical theology—and exorcism—from our seminaries, do we not now collect rotten fruit, such as (but certainly not limited to) the abuse crisis?

Woe to the Church if she does not acknowledge Satan, does not recognize his works, does not shed light in the devil's dark corners, as Jesus did.

Follow Jesus—do the same—is what Father Longenecker is saying.

It's also what Sister Lucia dos Santos of Fatima indicated when she warned of our era as one of "diabolical disorientation."

Open your eyes, your ears! Pray the "scales" away. Take a look backstage at what is *really* occurring in the world around us.

Too many in our seminaries, rectories, and dicasteries present the devil as an outdated product of philosophy or psychology. We have put the psychiatrist's couch where once was the confessional. We fear the label of "superstitious."

We have not the luxury of such thinking. The times are too dangerous for a solely theological approach. Like the angels, we must move swiftly. Like the angels who wage war, we must carry our swords into daily battle, resplendent with grace, and in the name of Jesus.

—Michael H. Brown
Palm Coast, Florida
March 11, 2020

Introduction

I live in South Carolina, where signs outside country churches remind you that "Jesus Saves." Complete strangers are likely to ask if you've been "born again" or have "a personal relationship with the Lord Jesus." Down south, the old-time religion is still emblazoned on billboards, preached from pulpits and radio shows. Television preachers still weep and rage and remind you that "Jesus' blood will wash away your sins" and that the Lord Jesus "died to take away the sins of the world."

I've always been sympathetic to the nonbeliever who hears this religious jargon, scratches his head, and really, honestly doesn't get it. He might well ask, "Excuse me, what exactly does that mean, 'Jesus saves'? What am I saved from? What is he saving?"

I sympathize when they ask, "What does a person executed for sedition in the backwater of the Roman Empire two thousand years ago have to do with me? How, exactly does his death take away the selfish things I've done, and were my 'sins' really so bad anyway? Hey, I've never murdered anybody!"

If this bewildered head scratcher encounters Catholic Christianity, he will become even more befuddled by what seems cryptic and creepy language. He hears, "This is my Body. This is my Blood. Unless you eat my Flesh and drink my Blood you do not have life within you." The priest solemnly pronounces, "Behold the Lamb of God who takes away the sins of the world," and if he listens carefully, the questioner will hear the priest mumbling about "this offering, this oblation, this sacrifice" or "this victim, this pure victim, this spotless victim."

Surely we can be sympathetic to the modern person who, having listened carefully, is more than bewildered. He is offended and asks, "We're talking about blood sacrifice here, right? We don't do that anymore. We don't sacrifice goats to the fertility goddess to have healthy babies and make the crops grow."

He might add, "Furthermore, if I am hearing you correctly, you're actually talking about *human* sacrifice. C'mon. We're not Neanderthals. We're not Aztecs, for goodness sake. We're not the wild-eyed, heart-plucking devotees of some primitive Hindu cult, like in the second Indiana Jones movie. What's all this blood-curdling talk about barbaric gods who need to be appeased with human sacrifice? Surely we're beyond such voodoo demon talk?"

I am not only sympathetic to anyone who asks such questions, but I am also convinced that most Christians of every persuasion would be hard-pressed to explain the religious language they take for granted. If they do try to explain it, they end up using other religious language that is just as mystifying. I have tried this from time to time—asking good Christians, "So how would you explain the phrase 'Jesus died to save you from your sins' to a non-Christian who doesn't have a clue what on earth you're talking about?"

The theological type will stroke his beard and say, "Yes, this requires an understanding of the doctrine of justification, which must be distinguished of course, from sanctification. Anselm's satisfaction theory must be compared to the penal substitution theory of atonement. These concepts could be elucidatory...."

The liturgical Christian might reply, "Through the Paschal Mystery we identify with the sacrifice in a sacramental way, and this identification and participation in that death grants us an inner renewal and participation in the resurrection event."

When pressed, the person in the pew might say, "Jesus died to save you from your sins? Well, what it means is that sin separates us from God, and Jesus takes care of that because, when He died He saved us from our sins, and we should die, but He died instead of us."

"OK, but how does that work? Is it some kind of magic? And you said He died instead of me, but I'm going to die anyway, so it's not really true, is it?"

There's a frustrating problem here. The very heart of the Christian Faith — the death and resurrection of Jesus Christ — has become obscured by religious language, customs, and concepts that mean virtually nothing to someone who has not been educated in that religion. Modern people don't get it. The death of Christ has become a stumbling block rather than a steppingstone. It's a wall, but it should be a door.

Even worse, because they are poorly catechized, an awful lot of Catholics have simply opted out of attempting an explanation. Once they started to think it through, they came up empty. They haven't stopped believing in God; they might even respect and believe in Jesus in some vague sort of way, but if they were asked to explain what the crucifix means or how Jesus' death has anything to do with them and their daily life, they'd come up with a mere shrug of the shoulders or a quizzical look.

In other words, they don't understand the phrases "Jesus died to save you from your sins" or "Behold the Lamb of God who takes away the sins of the world" any more than the befuddled non-Christian in the street.

Their confusion is understandable. In a utilitarian age, a practical people are right to wonder what the death of a criminal two thousand years ago has to do with them. In a scientific age, we wonder what ritual sacrifice has to do with our lives. In a hi-tech, seemingly civilized society, it is perfectly fair for people to be bewildered by religious notions linked with animal and especially human sacrifice. We are not primitive Stone Age people living in the jungle. Blood sacrifices seem barbaric, cruel, pointless, and superstitious.

This obstacle is nothing new. For the last 150 years or so, from the dawn of the modern age, religious thinkers have pondered the problem. How does one make sense of a Stone Age religion in a scientific age? How do miracles fit into a scientifically verifiable mentality, and what in heaven's name does a modern man with jet planes, iPhones, and the internet have to do with sacrificing goats, plucking out the beating heart of a sacrificial victim, or picking through a bull's intestines to prognosticate the future?

In the face of such a conundrum, the modernist answer has been to throw out all that superstitious, supernatural, sacrificial stuff as just a lot of worn-out religious junk.

"It was crude and primitive to start with, and it is now well past its 'sell-by' date. We know better. Let's clear out Grandma's ecclesiastical attic," the modernists argued.

Thus the campaign to reinterpret the Christian Faith began. The modernist Bible scholars stripped out all the miracle stories as you would cut out the rust from an old car. They salvaged the beautiful meanings and threw away the rest. So, for example, Jesus' miracle of feeding the five thousand was reinterpreted as a wonderful parable about sharing. Jesus walking on water? It became a beautiful story about having faith. But nobody really believes that He actually walked on water.

All that talk about sacrifice? We now know that Jesus did away with sacrifices at the Last Supper when he had a happy meal with His friends. The Holy Sacrifice of the Mass? That is really just a fellowship time during which we all gather around the table and sing campfire songs, such as "Give Peace a Chance," and then we hear a pep talk about how we should all be tolerant and kind and try to do something about immigrants and the environment. Sacrifice? That became a byword for giving a little bit more of your time, talent, and treasure in order to start a soup kitchen and make the world a better place.

They were desperate to make Christianity "relevant," so in addition to turning all the life-shattering events of the Gospels into charming fables and meaningful symbols, they also made Christianity "relevant" by emphasizing how good it would be for you. This is Christianity as therapy: "You should find Jesus, and He will help you with your addiction problem, your troublesome teens, your tired marriage, your grief, your unemployment — whatever." They sold Jesus like a snake oil salesman sells a cure-all ointment for everything from pimples to constipation.

This attempt to reinterpret the ancient religion was a disaster. It clipped the eagle's wings, castrated the bull, declawed the lion, and shot down angels in full flight. The ancient religion *did* need to be understood and reformulated, but what was needed was not this milquetoast reinterpretation. Rather what was needed was a fresh understanding of what Christ's sacrifice actually meant in the first place and what it means for modern people today. I actually believe the concept of sacrifice is more meaningful and powerful in its impact than ever before, and this book is my attempt to drive home not only what "sacrifice" means but also what it does.

To do this, it will be necessary for us to sacrifice a few sacred cows of our own. The religious language we use concerning sacrifice—"the Lamb of God who takes away the sins of the world" and "Jesus died to save you from your sins"—will have to be set aside for a time, not because they are untrue, but because, on their own, they are incomprehensible to many people. The traditional language of sacrifice originated in an ancient culture where blood sacrifices were an assumed part of everyday life. Sacrifice does have meaning for modern people, but to unlock that meaning, we will have to dive much deeper.

To understand phrases such as "being saved" or "Jesus takes away the sins of the world," we need to understand what the "sins of the world" are. First of all, please understand that, by "sins of the world," I am not referring to the naughty things you've done. All those selfish, petty, mean, and shameful thoughts, words, and deeds are merely the symptom of a deeper disease. To confront "the sins of the world," we have to penetrate the deepest realm of our humanity. We have to take a deep breath and plunge into the stark reality of evil. That dive will take us into the underworld where it is dark and cold and where "there be dragons."

This is not a theology book. I will not use theological language philosophical concepts, psychological terminology, academic arguments, or purely logical reasoning. This is because the depths into which we must venture are areas of the human heart and mind where a deeper kind of logic operates. It is the logic and language of the underworld. It is the labyrinth of dreams where the language is apocalyptic, and the images are mystical and mythical.

Therefore, be warned. As the inscription reads on the old maps, where the map ended and the terror began, "Here be dragons."

We will face some of the monsters that symbolize and reveal the complexity of evil. I'm thinking of those terrifying, alien-looking creatures that dwell in the darkest depths of the deepest ocean trench. I'm thinking of the hounds and hags of hell and beasts from beyond the darkest corners of our weirdest nightmares. I am using this type of language because I believe the imagination is a surer guide through the darkness than theoretical theologizing.

This journey will take us into the dark caves of Moria, into the realm of the Balrog and the orcs, Leviathan, Grendel, and the terrible dragon Tiamat. It will take us to wade through the foul-smelling marshes of Lerna — the gate of the underworld — to wrestle with the Hydra, that huge many-headed serpent with poisonous breath and blood so vile, even to smell it was to perish.

This is not theory or theoretical theology. If you read this book seriously, you will be shaken and troubled to the core.

We must go into those swamps and caves, for if Christianity is true, then it is the most astounding and revolutionary message ever to take humanity by the scruff of the neck and give it a good shake.

It is desperately important in our age to speak in these terms because our moral imagination, on the one hand, is weak, pale, and sickly, while ironically, in the realm of popular culture, the mythical imagination is healthier than ever. The academic world is a dry husk of learned articles filled with jargon and footnotes, while in the world of movies, television, gaming, and fantasy literature, the imagination roars and soars.

We must, therefore, use the imagination to dive like a spelunker into the depths of the underworld, then surface spluttering with joy, clutching the pearl of great price — which is to truly grasp the mysterious meaning of Christ's sacrifice. If we do not dive deeply, our faith will wither away into dry theological theories, warm sentimentality, and the horrible plague of utility. If we do not go on the quest to encounter the dragons of the deep, our faith will splutter out — ending not with a bang, but a whimper.

Immortal Combat

Modern Christianity has lost sight of its true purpose and mission. Twisted into political activism, therapeutic bromides, and sentimental, subjective devotions, infected with silly New Age self-help theories and weighed down with internal quarrels, immorality, and corruption, Christians are confused and bewildered—knocked sideways by the modern world with its strident ideologies and shallow solutions.

The only thing that will save us is to turn our back on the plastic Disneyland of the surface world and enter into the realms that lie beneath. There we will face the dark violence and deep deceptions of the human heart and come once again to the true meaning of this event at the center of time, which we recall with a crucifix.

The only thing that will save us is to contemplate the Cross, recognizing it as the turning point of history, the climax of the ancient conflict, and the ground of immortal combat. Our only hope is to grasp the true meaning of what happened on that hilltop outside Jerusalem two thousand years ago and to understand how it is more relevant and vital today than it has ever been. Then, once we have grasped it with our hearts and minds, it will be our task to grasp it with our whole being and take up that Cross as a drowning man would cling to a piece of wreckage.

Immortal combat means wrestling with the monsters of the deep. It is the way of a Christian Hercules who slaughters the Hydra with sword and fire. This way of the Christian warrior is a summons to all the baptized to first of all ponder the dread curse of evil and the full victory of the Cross, then to turn from our downward path and take up that Cross and follow Jesus Christ —Victim, Victor, and King of the Universe.

—Dwight Longenecker
October 31, 2019

Part 1

The Heart of Darkness

1

War in Heaven

Have you noticed that nobody sings "Onward, Christian Soldiers" anymore? I sang it as a kid in our Evangelical church. I still know the first verse:

> Onward, Christian soldiers,
> Marching as to war,
> With the Cross of Jesus
> Going on before.
> Christ the royal master
> Leads against the foe
> Forward into battle, see His banners go!
> Onward, Christian soldiers!

Go ahead. Look through any modern, up-to-date hymnbook. You won't find it. Nor will you find "Fight the Good Fight with All Thy Might" or "Soldiers of Christ, Arise." Good luck finding any of the old hymns about Christian warfare. The editors have quietly removed them, censored them out, consigned them to the cupboard with the plumed hat, the cape, the dusty armor, and the rusty swords.

We don't talk like that anymore. We don't sing rousing military marching songs. Instead we rise up on eagles' wings, and Jesus hears us crying in the night, and there is only one set of footprints on the beach because that's when He carried us. We haven't beaten our swords into plowshares; we've beaten them into pacifiers.

The problem with this puppy-dogs-and-kittens Christianity is that it is not really Christianity. From the beginning to the end of time, the heart of the old, old story is not comfort, but conflict.

One of the most important verses in the Bible is hidden away right at the end in the book of Revelation:

> Then war broke out in heaven; Michael and his angels battled against the dragon. The dragon and its angels fought back, but they did not prevail and there was no longer any place for them in heaven. The huge dragon, the ancient serpent, who is called the Devil and Satan, who deceived the whole world, was thrown down to earth, and its angels were thrown down with it. (12:7–9)

This passage refers not to the end of time, but the beginning. The war in heaven took place before the history of our planet. Lucifer was cast down with his cohort and imprisoned here. Earth became the silent planet—a dark dungeon ruled by Satan. This is the foundation of the story we all need to understand. This earth became the domain of Satan and his dark angels. They chose to rebel against God, and so they were cast down, alienated forever and imprisoned here.

Then God established a plan to re-take this planet. To reclaim it, He needed to outwit the maleficent Lord of the World. He would do this by creating His own secret agents—creatures so humble that the proud spirit Satan could never in a million years have envisioned them.

Rather than creating another order of spirit beings such as angels, God created a new species—both physical and spiritual at once. Neither ape nor angel, these creatures would be called "humans" because they came from the clay of the earth. The word "human" comes from the Latin word *humus*, meaning "earth." It is the same word from which we derive the words "humility" and "humor," and the fact that "Adam" also means "earth" matches neatly. Creating humans out of the dust of the earth was one of God's great jokes.

It was one of God's simple strokes of genius. This humble creature would be fully physical like the animals, but it would also gaze in wonder at a newborn child, make music, poems, and paintings; it would play games, invent tools, laugh and cry, dance and sing and wonder at the stars, and—worst of all for the Proud One—it would learn to love and worship God Himself.

Satan spotted these new creatures, and he saw at once what God had done. Immediately he hated the new half-breeds with an intense and hellish contempt. He gnashed his teeth with rage. He transmogrified into a dragon and snorted volcanic fire and smoke. He folded his leathery wings, strutted, preened, and paced with frustration and fury. He could not understand why God had created these mongrels and what purpose they could possibly serve, but out of the sheer malice in his heart, he was determined to claim them as his own. He would enslave them, he would torture them, and eventually he would devour them.

You might say I am spinning a fairy tale. I don't mind. I happen to think fairy tales are often truer than facts. The story of Satan's fall is the legacy of the war which has, for four thousand years, been the foundation of the Faith—the lens through which we have understood God's great gamble. But we, in our lily-livered age, apathetic in our affluence and cowardly in our comfortable lives, have studiously avoided the language of war. We are frightened of offending others. Timid in the face of Muslim jihadis, we turn away from the idea of battle. We are embarrassed by the whole idea of the "Church Militant" and wish The Salvation Army would change its name.

We also turn away from the idea of spiritual warfare because we have been told that Satan doesn't really exist. We are told he is "the projection of the negativities from the collective unconscious." He has become a nightmare but nothing more, frightening to be sure, but no more real than the bogeyman, the monster under the bed, Godzilla, or the Creature from the Black Lagoon.

C. S. Lewis reminded us that Lucifer likes nothing more than for us to disbelieve in his existence, and yet immortal combat against the dark forces has been the mainstay of mankind's spiritual story.

A wizened Lutheran bishop in the 1930s named Gustav Aulen wrote a little book called *Christus Victor*, which reminded all of us that from the beginning, the entire story of salvation was understood as a cosmic battle. There was not only war in heaven, but that war continued on this darkened planet earth. Satan and his cohort were locked in an everlasting conflict against the Almighty, and, in his pride, Satan would never surrender. He would rather stew forever in the fetid, boiling sewage of hell than surrender.

Earth is the battlefield, and the human race is caught up in that battle. This is total war, and every human being, in one way or another, is caught up in the cosmic conflict, whether he likes it or not. Every human being will have to take sides. Every human being, by virtue of being one of God's special half-breeds, is fighting either for heaven or for hell. There are no neutral territories. There are no pacifists.

We all must choose, and not to choose is to choose. To pretend the forces of evil do not exist is ostrich-head-in-sand idiocy. You only need to read yesterday's headlines to know in the pit of your stomach that an evil greater than mere human weakness and mistakes exists in the world. To stand on the sidelines and watch the battle is to be on the side of Satan, because all it takes for evil to triumph is for enough good men to do nothing.

Furthermore, to choose means a one hundred percent commitment. There is no room for Saturday-afternoon soldiers. This is not a dress rehearsal or one of those Civil War reenactments where we study strategies, wear a costume, and fire blanks at our friends for fun before sitting down to a picnic lunch.

If you know your Bible history, you will remember that from the beginning, war is the plot, and war is the purpose. The Bible is not a collection of sentimental stories about people who discovered a wonderful spirituality. It is not a compilation of inspirational sayings or a compendium of the world's wisdom. It is not a manifesto for political action or a master plan to make the world into some sort of artificial utopia like that town in the movie, *The Truman Show*. It is not an anthology of lovely stories of pious people who sang about raindrops on roses and whiskers on kittens.

It is the chronicle of war. It is the record of brutal, seemingly endless cosmic combat taking place in the gritty reality of human history.

Make a list of those Old Testament characters. They were warriors. Father Abraham gathered over three hundred soldiers and marched out to rescue his nephew, Lot, from the kings who had sacked Sodom. Moses led the Israelites in war. Joshua fought the battle of Jericho. Jael put a tent peg through Sisera's head, Samson slew hundreds with the jawbone of an ass, and Deborah, Gideon, Jephthah, and Saul set out to conquer the Philistines. David fought Goliath, and Elijah slaughtered all the prophets of Baal, and not one of them escaped him.

Immortal Combat

Read the psalms again, and notice how many of them refer to battles against the enemy. Here is a war song of King David for instance:

> Blessed be the Lord, my rock,
>> who trains my hands for battle,
>> my fingers for war;
> My safeguard and my fortress,
>> my stronghold, my deliverer,
> My shield, in whom I take refuge,
>> who subdues peoples under me. (Ps. 144:1–2)

Let's face it, the Old Testament makes for a pretty violent read, and the history of the Church is not without its bloodshed. Whether it is the Crusades, the purge of the Albigensians, the Thirty Years' War, the battles of Lepanto and Vienna, or the beheadings, tortures, and burnings at the stake of martyrs and suspected martyrs, the history of our religion is one of war.

What are we to make of it? Shall we glorify such bloodshed? I think not. But being embarrassed by our violent past has led us to step away from militant language. Jesus the Meek has become the icon of our age. Yes, He was meek, but He was also militant. How did He do that? Simple. He was militant in His meekness. He was both victim and victor. He entered immortal combat. He was a herculean hero—a warrior priest.

So what shall we do? Launch a new crusade? Shall we bomb abortion clinics and assassinate our enemies? Shall the Knights of Columbus exchange their ceremonial sabers for assault rifles, their plumed hats and sashes for helmets, camouflage, and combat boots? Of course not. I am not aiming to start a Catholic Jihadist movement, nor am I calling for a return to the scaffold and the stake.

But I am calling for the baptized to realize that all of us are called to be warriors, not wimps.

Some might imagine that once Jesus came onto the scene, He ended all that military language in favor of being a flower child. But He understood from the start that He was in the front line of battle. That's why, immediately after His baptism, He went into the desert to do battle with His ancient foe.

He recognized immediately who His real enemies were and called them out as a brood of vipers, hypocrites, sons of Satan, liars, and murderers. He said clearly that He did not come to bring peace but a sword, that he would baptize with fire, and following Him would mean separation from wife and children, mothers and fathers. To join Him is to join the forces of light against the powers of darkness.

Nor does it end there. St. Peter and St. Paul take up the charge of the light brigade and use militant language throughout their epistles. Peter says our adversary the devil is like a roaring lion stalking about, seeking whom he may devour. Paul tells Timothy to "endure hardship as a good soldier of Jesus Christ and put on the full armor of God and stand firm against the wily plots of the devil." The apostles do battle against heretics, hypocrites, false teachers, and charlatans of every kind, and their language is sharp and clear.

Find a saint, and you will find a warrior. Virtually every saint mentions the spiritual battle — even the little girls. St. Thérèse of Lisieux cries out, "Sanctity! It must be won at the point of a sword!" And on her deathbed she says, "I will die with my weapons in my hand!" St. Benedict trained his monks to be soldiers in the great battle, as did Sts. Francis Xavier, Padre Pio, Maximilian Kolbe, and every saint who didn't merely write about battle, but lived the battle. They would not be saints without heroic virtue, and they would not have attained heroic virtue without warfare.

The problem with military language, however, is that we too often go into battle unprepared. We aren't really sure who we are fighting against or how to engage in the battle. We are untrained in our weaponry, our armor is rusty, and we are out of shape. The strife is fierce and the warfare long, and, being confused by the tricks of the enemy, we often lash out against the wrong foe. Too often we attack the soldiers on our own side, bringing them down with friendly fire, or we attack our allies thinking they are the enemy simply because they wear a different uniform.

This is stupid and disastrous and exactly what our real enemy wants us to do. Instead, to do battle successfully, we must first gather our intelligence. To defeat the enemy, we must know the enemy. To fight successfully, we must understand his strategies. To be victorious, we must first understand the true darkness and depth of the depravity we face.

We talk about spiritual warfare but have not considered who or what we are truly fighting against. Perhaps we imagine we are amateur exorcists, praying the Rosary with furrowed brow and tired fingers. Good. Pray the Rosary, but why are you praying it, and what do you hope to accomplish? To make headway, we must first face the depths. The evil we are battling is not just human selfishness, lust, rage, and greed. These are symptoms of a deeper illness in our race. There are darker monsters in the caves where our ancestors slept.

I call this deeper darkness the Sin of the World, for it is not simply the evil things we've done, but an evil that is twisted in and around and through the very foundations of the world. The Sin of the World is an insidious parasitic worm lodged deep in the very viscera of the world itself. It dozes, satiated and smug in the underground caverns of the heart. There Smaug himself—the great reptile—lies in wait.

To understand the enemy, we must first understand that, like every serpent, he slithers and hides. He is not obvious, and he wears many disguises. He is not easy to identify. Indeed, he is so subtle in his camouflage and subterfuge that we are usually blind to his real identity, and he remains invisible.

Because he is a shape-shifter, we will study his ways by studying the mythical, monstrous forms he has taken—and the first monster we will look at is the Minotaur.

2

The Minotaur and the Labyrinth

In Spain the huge black bull stumbles into the ring. There, before the cheering crowd, the matador — that curious cross between a ballet dancer and a sword fighter — engages in a duel to the death with El Toro. Like some ancient horned beast of the underworld, the black bull — virile and snorting with rage — is lured to his death.

How strange that the bull was worshipped across the ancient world! From the ghostly images on the walls of the caves of Lascaux, to the constellation Taurus in the stars, the bull was a sacred beast.

Among the Mesopotamians, Egyptians, and Minoans, images, masks, and idols of the bull god abound. Whether it is the huge bulls wandering the streets of Kolkata or the golden calf worshipped by the Hebrews in the wilderness, the bull became an image of the divine. Not only was it considered a kind of god, but bulls were the supreme animal of sacrifice. On the altars of Baal, Mithras, Marduk, Jupiter, or Jahweh, the bulls would be offered and slaughtered.

Why the bull? Why did they worship the golden calf? Because the bull represents potency and power. He stands for all that is earthbound, earthy, and strong. The gold is the worldly wealth they worshipped, and the horns of the black bull hint at that other horned god—the Lord of Lust and Darkness, Balrog, Baal, and Beelzebub himself.

I proposed that to understand how Jesus saves, we must first understand the true nature of evil. To understand evil, we must face the Minotaur. If the black bull stands for the drooling, lusting, potent demons of the dark, then the Minotaur stands for the terrifying hybrid of the demonic and the human, for if you remember the myths, the Minotaur is a beastly blend of man and bull. A muscular giant with the head of a bull, the Minotaur is the horrible, snorting result of a queen named Pasiphaë who, in her panting lust, mated with a bull.

Asterion is the Minotaur's name. He has the virile power of the bull combined with the intelligence and pride of man. He blends the brute strength and malice of the bull with the cunning deception of a cruel and violent man. At once stubborn and aggressive, he is at the same time shrewd and brutally handsome. Most intriguing of all, Asterion the Minotaur is hidden in the dark.

In the ancient myth, Minos the king has locked Asterion in the labyrinth—a network of passageways beneath the royal palace. The subterranean maze is made up of confusing corridors that turn and return on themselves—hallways that lead into cul-de-sacs and doors that open into empty rooms. In the center lurks the Minotaur ready to murder anyone who dares to confront him.

The citizens of Athens had killed King Minos's son. To make reparation for his death and avoid the terrible plague, the Athenians send seven young men and seven maidens to the palace of Minos to be sacrificed to the Minotaur in the labyrinth below the palace. The hero Theseus, aided by the princess Ariadne, sets out to penetrate the labyrinth, rescue the young people, and kill Asterion.

The Minotaur and the Labyrinth

The ancients understood that the real evil in the world lurks deep beneath the surface. The ancient mythmakers knew that beneath the glittering palaces of worldly power there were bull-ish beasts. They knew that beneath the king's chambers, bright with morning light and filled with earthly delights, the Minotaur was lurking in the labyrinth. Indeed, they understood that the king's treasures, his sumptuous banquets, his courtly courtiers and lovely ladies were all built over the labyrinth, derived from the demonic powers of the underworld.

That is why Asterion the Minotaur lives in the center of the labyrinth right below the royal palace. He is the beast bellowing below. He is the heart of evil beating beneath the shimmering surface, the drooling lust throbbing in the heat beneath the cool facade.

In the first half of this book we are considering the Sin of the World in detail, but the Sin of the World cannot be discovered as long as we stay in the king's palace. The palace is a place of good manners and nice people. The king's courtiers do not seem evil. Indeed, they seem very good. They are busy about the king's business. They are educated and urbane. They are well dressed, well connected, and well-to-do. They live and laugh on the surface, and if we stay in the palace with them, we can continue to exist on that delightful surface level.

It is tempting to stay in the palace. Not only are the people wealthy, kind, and charming, but they seem to be doing good things in the kingdom. Perhaps they are building hospitals and schools. Certainly they are feeding the poor and improving the water supply. They are helping the homeless and raising money for worthy causes. It seems good to stay in the marble palace.

So it is with the surface life of the majority of believers. They stay in the palace of the Church with nice people doing nice things to make the world a nicer place. They never approach the entrance to the subterranean labyrinth. They ignore the roars of the Minotaur, and as long as they do, they will never truly enter the battle. They will remain in the silken palace where all is comfortable and smooth.

However, in the labyrinth below, Asterion the Minotaur still bellows. Notice that the word "minotaur" is a blend of the king's own name, Minos, and *taur*, which means "bull." In other words, the Minotaur is the bestial side of the king himself, and it is the king who has imprisoned Asterion in the labyrinth below. This is what we ourselves do: we deny our demons. We hide our shameful secret sins and lock away the evil creatures of the night. This is what we do as individuals, as families, as a Church, and as a society.

Therefore, if we want to engage in the conflict, like Theseus, we must leave the palace and the lovely Ariadne to venture into the chambers below and navigate that monster-infested labyrinth, which is the subterranean maze of the human mind and heart.

Why would we do this? To save the innocent youths and maidens, for the evil ones in the world, like the Minotaur, are always hungry to devour the innocent. That is one of the marks of the Beast.

As we set off, however, we will soon learn that the labyrinth is not only the lower level of the world. It is our underworld, too. Beneath our surface life there is a cavern, a cellar, a dark and bewildering labyrinth. Each of us has our own Minotaur — the fearsome blend of the man and the beast in us. Deep below the surface, the wild things lurk in each of our hearts.

Be warned. Within your own mind and heart Asterion awaits.

What will we find as we descend into the underworld? This is not just any maze. It is devised with the most amazing cunning.

It is a complicated network of smoke and mirrors—a world of false images, lies, and deception.

Nothing is what it seems, for everything here is a lie. You thought that was a door? No, it was the reflection of a door. There is nothing there. Did you think that light at the end of the passage was the way to follow? It was put there to fool you. If you follow it, you will fall into a pit full of vipers. Did you think that floor was solid and sure? It is quicksand.

This labyrinth is full of traps. You enter what seems to be a banquet hall housing a table laden with a sumptuous feast, but the food turns out to be rotten and crawling with worms. Did you hear the lovely ladies singing in a room far, far away? Follow the sirens, and before your eyes they will turn into harpies, foul crones muttering incantations for your destruction. This is the labyrinth you must navigate to find the Minotaur—and then when you do find him beware. He may have changed his appearance, seeming to be a charming gentleman. He will offer you all the kingdoms of the world. He will lure you further into the trap, for he is a liar and a manifestation of the Father of Lies.

I am taking the time to explain what is before you because, in the chapters that follow, you will feel at times that you are, indeed, in a labyrinth. You will need to tread through corridors of the mind and deceptions of the heart. What I will lay before you will seem too extreme. You will feel depressed and bewildered. You will be tempted to close your eyes, put the book aside, dismiss what I have written, and return to the palace above where everything is sumptuous and comfortable, clean and neat.

Do not give in. Stay with the battle. In the chapters that follow, we will peel away layer upon layer of deception, subterfuge, and lies. You may become confused. You will doubt and even deny what you read. That, of course, is exactly what you would expect in the labyrinth. Confusion and fear are the emotions you ought to feel when facing a monster like the Minotaur.

Finally, when you face the heart of evil, you will quake with fear because you realize that not only has Asterion been imprisoned in the labyrinth, but he has also chosen to hide there, and he hates to be exposed. You will see that beneath the luxurious palaces of the king is the Minotaur, and if you discover his lair, he will greet you with red-eyed hatred. Like the black bull in the arena, he will eye you and paw the ground, full of rage. Stubborn and strong, snorting and roaring, he will charge.

In the labyrinth we will encounter other mythical beasts from the underworld, and each one will reveal new layers of deception by the Lord of the Flies, the Father of Lies.

Before we go down into the labyrinth we must travel back in time to the very beginning to see how the Dragon, the Dark Lord in serpentine form, did his work in Eden.

We have to start at the beginning.

We have to get back to the Garden.

3

The Dragon in the Garden

An exorcist told me something I will never forget. He said the ministry of exorcism is dirty, disgusting, and exhausting work. A real exorcism, he said, is knock-down, bare-knuckle, snarling, hand-to-hand combat with the devil. You fight amidst the stench of hell, and worst of all is the fact that you lose track of where you are. You seem to be in a wilderness with no points of reference. There is no logic or reasoning. Nothing can be predicted and planned. You're wrestling on quicksand; everything slips and slides. There is no foothold. It is like grappling with an octopus in oil in the dark.

Why? Because the devil is a liar. He lies constantly. He plays a part. He might snarl and hiss one moment or whine and howl the next, but it's an act. He's lying. The demon may cower in fear and whimper and say he is going to his appointed place in hell, but he's lying. He does nothing but lie. It is as if his whole personality is an extraordinarily complex network of lies as deep as the pits of hell and as vast as the everlasting dark.

If the first thing a warrior must know is the enemy, then understand that this enemy is a liar. Jesus Christ recognized him and said he was not only the Father of Lies, but he was "a murderer from the beginning, ... and there is no truth in him" (John 8:44).

In other words, he not only lies; he is the Untruth. His realm is chaos and destruction.

Since the enemy is the Father of Lies, be prepared to face the most expert and subtle liar the universe has ever known. He is the charming Mefistofele—a gentleman caller who makes you an offer you can't refuse. That sly murderer appeared in paradise, and that is where the battle with the ancient worm tongue commences.

You remember the story: God created Adam and Eve and placed them in the Garden of Eden. They were naked as newborns, innocent and free. They were permitted to eat the fruit of the Tree of Life, but they were forbidden to eat the fruit of the Tree of the Knowledge of Good and Evil.

They were given a choice, and locked into this gift of a choice is the riddle that lies at the heart of mankind's destiny. Here lies the basic code by which we can understand the ground rules of immortal combat. The simple and terrifying fact is that God gave Adam and Eve a choice. He gave them free will. The freedom to choose may seem simple and elementary, but it is also terrifying because its implications are eternal.

We take choice for granted. We make choices every day, but we rarely consider how astonishing it is that we have choice at all. Stop for a moment and consider: embedded in this power to choose is a little red spark called "desire." The story states it clearly: "When the woman saw that the fruit of the tree was good for food and pleasing to the eye, she desired it for it would give her wisdom." Desire is the engine of choice. We gaze at the options, and we desire one thing more than another. Desire drives us to choose.

Do not be mistaken; desire, of itself, is not evil. At an instinctive level, desire is simply the need for food, shelter, safety, security, and love. We are born with an innocent longing for everything that is beautiful, good, and true. Desire is also the built-in yearning for God Himself, for He is the source and summit of all that is beautiful, good, and true.

This is getting complicated.

Stop to think it through.

It's important for what follows.

We desire all that which is beautiful, good, and true, and because we have free will we are able to choose that which is beautiful, good, and true. This desire and this ability to choose are themselves good. However, by its very nature, the power to choose what is good must include the possibility of choosing that which is *not* good — otherwise, there would be no choice.

Making a choice, then, automatically brings with it the knowledge of good and evil. Why? Because when you choose one thing over another, you have decided the thing you have chosen is better than the thing you did not choose.

Let me give you an example. Let us say you are a primitive person in the jungle, and you are hungry. You have before you an orange and a flat rock the size and shape of your hand. You must choose.

If you choose the orange because you are hungry and it is juicy and sweet, then you have decided that the orange is better than the rock. If you choose the rock because you might make a weapon from it with which to hunt, you have decided that the rock is better than the orange. Suddenly, for the first time (because you perceive one thing to be better than the other), you have understood that there is such a thing as good and evil. From this knowledge of good and evil humanity begins to develop a sense of morality.

Why did God forbid the knowledge of good and evil? Because He wanted his new creatures to remain innocent and immortal, desiring and choosing only that which was beautiful, good, and true. But the possibility of choosing evil had to be part of the equation. There was no other way. You could not freely choose the good without the possibility of choosing evil.

But there was a deeper reason for the drama. God wanted His newborn creatures to have a choice so they could choose to love Him freely. Love must be chosen. It cannot be forced. If love is forced it is not love. Therefore, without choice there is no evil, but without choice there is also no love.

This, therefore, was God's great gamble. He must have love because He is Love, but love must be chosen. And for it to be chosen, there must be an option *not* to love. Therefore, God gave His children the power to choose, and with the power to choose comes the possibility of choosing poorly. Once Adam and Eve made their choice, they did, indeed, receive the knowledge of good and evil.

The Father of Lies was pleased with this. He wanted the human creatures to have the knowledge of good and evil so that he could draw them away from their Maker, manipulate, dominate, enslave, and destroy them. The way he would do this was by distorting their desire.

Notice how the suave serpent deceived them. First, he asked Eve whether it was true that God said they were not to eat the fruit of that particular tree. He hooks her with a question, and through her curiosity he sparks her desire for what was forbidden. Once her desire for the deadly fruit is sparked with a seemingly innocent question, the dragon presents the blatant lie: "You will not surely die!" With this lie, he proposes that God is a liar. Then having put in the knife, he twists it.

"God knows if you eat from the Tree of the Knowledge of Good and Evil you will be like Him." In other words, you will have what He has and become who He is. With the twist of the knife, the serpent twists Eve's desire. What was an innocent desire for all that was beautiful, good, and true suddenly becomes a selfish desire — the desire to have something that belongs to another.

At the heart of our humanity, our innocent desire has been distorted. The "knowledge of good and evil" means that our desire flares up when someone else has what we want. We desire that good thing not only because it is good, but because someone else has it. Furthermore, we covet that object simply *because* the other person has it. Even worse, we often want that object not even for the sake of the object itself, but simply so that the other person cannot have it.

In the third and final *Lord of the Rings* film, *The Return of the King*, we witness the corruption of Gollum. In a flashback, we see that he is a hobbit named Smeagol. While fishing, his cousin Deagol finds the Ring of Power. Smeagol sees it and instantly desires it. The desire overwhelms him, and he kills Deagol to take it for himself. "Give it to us!" He snarls, "We wants it!"

Not only do we desire the object that another possesses, but, beating like a heart within the simple desire for the object, is a desire to be like the person who has what we want. We not only want what they have; we want what they are — in fact, to grab what they are, to devour them, consume them completely. That is why Smeagol kills his cousin — not only to take the ring, but to obliterate his rival and take his place.

And sure enough, this is the very temptation the ancient dragon offers Eve. He plants the idea within her mind that they could be like God. "If you eat from the tree, you will be like Him." And if they could be like Him, they would take his place. The ultimate way to take the rival's place requires that the rival be destroyed.

This is an unthinkable and shocking concept, and if the Father of Lies had stated it openly, they would have rejected such a thought not only as blasphemous and horrifying, but ridiculous. Instead he plants the seed of the idea in their hearts and minds without stating it bluntly. He does not say, "Go ahead and take the fruit. Take God's place, and by taking His place, eliminate Him forever!"

Instead, the devil simply suggests the idea: "If you eat of the fruit you will be like Him."

Thus the first seed of "imitation desire" is planted in their hearts and minds. What is imitation desire? It is the desire not only to have what belongs to our rival, but to be *like* the rival, to become someone greater — not only to take what they have, but to take what they are and finally to destroy them and take their place.

Study this concept. Look at it with a hard and steady glare. Meditate on this fact. The sin was not in eating a piece of fruit. The sin was not in yielding to sexual temptation. The sin was not even simply disobedience. Adam and Eve reached out, infected with the desire to be like God. By taking the fruit, they became their own little god and goddess. They ate the fruit, and the sweet juice of omnipotence dripped down their chin. They could be like God! They could be His rival! The great stone doors of the universe rumbled open before them. They could do as they pleased now. They had power!

And as they savored this new feeling in awe and wonder, the devil danced with delight.

Notice how the Father of Lies deceived Adam and Eve, but did so not with a simple lie, but by twisting the truth. This is always his tactic. He took the foundational truth about human nature and twisted it into the foundation of their destruction.

The essential truth of their creation is that they were, indeed, created in God's image to start with. They did not need to become like God, for they were already like Him. In their innocence they were rightly ordered toward their Creator and were in His image as a work of art is in the image of the artist. They reflected His image as the moon shines by the light of the sun. The serpent's temptation was for them to be the sun itself.

Greed, envy, and covetousness are the simple fruits of our distorted desire, but this imitation desire is the darker dragon. It is the engine of all the dark desires. It is the force from which they emanate. "For from the heart come evil thoughts, murder, adultery, unchastity, theft, false witness, blasphemy" (Matt. 15:19).

This, therefore, is the heart of darkness at the foundation of all things. This is the seed of the Sin of the World out of which all other evil grows. This imitation desire is the instinctual longing to be our own god and to destroy all rivals.

It is vital to realize that by its very nature, this sin is hidden from us. Imitation desire is rooted in the depths of our souls, deeper than our immediate awareness. This desire to be like God is buried deeper than our own breath. It is woven into who we are and into everything we think, say, and do. It is the basic assumption. It is the air we breathe. It is the way we are wired, and yet we are blind to it. We do not see it as the fish does not see the water. Should this heart of darkness be revealed to us, we would deny, deflect, and defend ourselves from that reality.

"Humankind cannot bear very much reality."[1]

This imitation desire is the secret hidden from the foundation of the world. This dark secret—that we believe ourselves to be

---

[1] T.S. Eliot, "Burnt Norton."

the center of the universe, our own little deity — is also the root of our soiled relationships. All human conflict stems from the simple fact that each one of us operates from within the basic assumption that we are the omnipotent One — the ruler and Lord of all things.

From this fundamental deception grows all the violence in the world, for we cannot all be omnipotent, and human history is, therefore, the history of the sons and daughters of Adam and Eve murdering one another.

"You surely shall not die!" The ancient worm tongue sweetly sang.

Liar.

Father of Lies. A murderer from the beginning, and there is no truth in him.

·

4

The Three-Headed Hound of Hell

There is a monster in one of the Harry Potter films that the author borrowed from hell. Hagrid calls the beast "Fluffy," but his real name is Cerberus — the three-headed hound from hell. Cerberus is not only an unholy, three-headed, howling attack dog, but he also has a serpent for a tail. In Greek myths Cerberus guards the gates of hell. Like the meanest junkyard dog imaginable, he lunges to devour anyone who tries to escape.

In the cosmic battle, Cerberus is one of the beasts from the underworld who needs to be slain. What do his three heads represent? They stand for three snarling, drooling consequences of the disastrous choice in Eden.

The first howling head of Cerberus represents power.

We have seen how the ancient dragon tempted our first parents. Through his cunning lies, their desire was distorted. They chose poorly. Their eyes were opened, and they immediately experienced the reality of good and evil. The first result of their choice was that they understood for the first time they had power. Real power. With free will comes power, and making a choice puts that power into gear and makes it real.

When He granted His creatures free will, God shared with them a small measure of His own power. Because I can make real choices, I have power, and furthermore, this power seems to be an integral part of who I am. It is not just that I *have* power. It feels like I *am* power, and I assume that the exercise of my power is justified.

This is a basic instinct. It is a key to survival. It is unquestioned. I, therefore, see nothing wrong with exercising my power to its greatest extent. To do as I please is as elementary as the need to breathe, eat, and drink, to procreate and live. It never once occurs to me that my will should be curtailed and my power limited in any way.

Furthermore, because I have the power to choose, my choice must be the right choice. I must be right. There can be no other option.

The total conviction that *I am right* is the heart of pride, and pride is the second head of the hell hound Cerberus.

We often confuse pride with vanity or arrogance. Vanity is taking undue pleasure in ourselves—our appearance, our accomplishments, our possessions, or our power. Arrogance is the strutting, boastful face of pride. It is a know-it-all attitude combined with an aggressive posture. Vanity and arrogance are outward indicators of pride, but they are no more than masks.

Real pride is the overwhelming, underlying, unshakeable, unchallenged, unquestioned, total, and complete conviction that *I am right*. Like power, pride is rooted in the ability to choose and the knowledge of good and evil.

It works like this: when I make a choice, I claim power for myself, but also, when I make a choice, I assume the choice I have made is the *right* choice. This conviction that *I am right* operates at the level of instinct. The very act of choosing includes the assumption that *I am right*. If I chose the orange instead of the rock I must have made the right choice. That is why I chose the orange: because I was convinced it was the right choice!

Pride is the total, complete, foundational assumption, before all else and above all else, that *I am right*, that my choices are right, that my beliefs are right, that my decisions are right, that everything I do is right. This complete conviction that *I am right* is deeply rooted in my character.

Therefore, as soon as I exercise power and make a choice, pride — the underlying belief that *I am right* — sneaks through the door.

Furthermore, power and pride are so basic and deeply embedded in the foundations of who we are that we cannot see them. Power and pride seem like part of the genetic code. They are the air we breathe. They are the world we live in. They are the foundation of the house, and foundations, by their very nature, are buried. They are deep down. They are invisible.

This invisibility of power and pride reveals the third head of Cerberus: prejudice.

Prejudice is intertwined with pride and power. To have a prejudice is to prejudge. It means our perceptions are biased: we view the world through tinted glasses. We do not judge objectively, but rather, we approach life's challenges with our ideas and opinions preloaded.

Power allows us to choose, and pride assumes that our choice was the right choice. Therefore, everything in life, from the lunch menu to the news headlines, comes to us through our preexisting assumptions that we have chosen well, that we are right. Our opinions about the world, relationships, religion and morals, politics and money — about everything — are already partially determined by the choices we have made and the pride by which we firmly believe that we have chosen well and that we are right.

Furthermore, prejudice poisons our relationships because if my choices are right, then the people who choose differently must be wrong. Power and pride automatically demand that the person who is different from me and who has chosen differently must be wrong—and if wrong, then bad.

Power, pride, and prejudice are the three heads of Cerberus. Like an unholy trinity, power, pride, and prejudice are interdependent: three heads, one foul beast called Ego. Power feeds pride, then power and pride feed prejudice. Together they make up the base level of our personalities, lives, and relationships.

Picture, then, this three-headed, slavering hound of hell. See the gigantic beast with the serpent's tail, his maws dripping with blood. That is human nature—growling with power, howling with pride, prowling with prejudice.

Study this beast from a safe distance. Cerberus guards the gates of the underworld. He keeps the souls from escaping, but he also keeps us from going into our own underworld—the deep places of our lives where the wild things are. Our power, pride, and prejudice prevent us from going there. We tell ourselves that we are good. We are right, and others are wrong, so we don't need to go into the depths. Cerberus keeps us out.

Examine the beast even more closely. Lying deep within each of us—both male and female—are what the archeologists of the soul tell us are the *animus* and the *anima*. The *animus* is the masculine aspect of our personality, made up of power, pride, and prejudice, the aggressive alpha males. They are the wolves within.

Beware your adversary Cerberus, who stalks around seeking whom he may devour. His three heads are the ugly side of our masculine nature, present in both men and women but displayed differently according to our complementary natures.

"Whoa!" you might say. "This makes us sound like hellish monsters to be sure! Are we really so prejudiced, proud, and power hungry as all that? Surely not."

I agree. We have learned to behave ourselves. The infant asserts his pride and power from the very beginning, but he soon learns that his power is limited, and his pride is deflated. The infant's power very soon bumps up against those with greater power. His power is circumscribed by circumstances beyond his control. His pride is limited because he soon learns that he has a lot to learn. But these corrections do not change his fundamental condition.

The power, pride, and prejudice are still lurking. They have not gone away. They have gone into hiding.

This is why Cerberus, like the Minotaur, is a creature of the underworld. Cerberus lurks in the darkness, beneath the surface of our ordinary world. He waits in his lair—always watchful and never sleeping. On the surface we may have learned that our power, pride, and prejudice are limited, but the three-headed hound is not dead. He has only been tossed a few bits of meat to keep him quiet.

We soon learn that to live together with others, power, pride, and prejudice must be suppressed. We have to keep Cerberus on a leash. Family, society, education, and religion all provide the leash we need. We are taught self-control. We learn that it is unacceptable to exercise raw, selfish power. We come to understand that we cannot assert our instinct to be "right" all the time. The members of society teach us to put our prejudices aside and experience life more objectively and to be more open-minded.

Unfortunately, these efforts only meet with limited success. Cerberus might be on a leash, but it's not a very strong leash, and Cerberus is a very strong beast. This is where Satan steps in. The dragon doesn't want his pet beast to be on a leash. He wants Cerberus to run wild, wreaking havoc. However, he knows this will be unacceptable in human society, so he does what he does best: he gets us to disguise the beast. He teaches us how to dress Cerberus up as a cuddly puppy.

In other words, we practice deception. We disguise our plots for power. We dress our pride up in an acceptable costume. We do a magician's trick with our prejudice. In all sorts of ways, we sugarcoat our power, pride, and prejudice. Instead of exercising raw power, we manipulate others. We accomplish our own ends while pretending we are helping them. Instead of raw pride and prejudice we pretend to be open-minded, tolerant, and accepting of other people and their ideas, while all the time the conviction burns within that we alone are right and good.

Like the Father of Lies himself, we weave deception into deception, and the person we deceive most effectively is ourself. After covering up our power, pride, and prejudice through manipulation and pretense, we then tell ourselves that we were right and good to do so, and thus the second deception consolidates the first. Since we are now priding ourselves on our effective deception, a downward spiral begins, and we believe ourselves to be even more right and good because that deception was also effective.

Cerberus may be on a leash, but it is an extending leash that actually allows him to run free. The frightening thing is not only that he runs free, but also, because of the very nature of power, pride, and prejudice, we are blind to the fact. We can't really see Cerberus. All we can see is the puppy disguise.

There is one final deception that is the granddaddy of them all. This is the self-deception that conceals the power, pride, and prejudice so effectively that we are forever blind to their existence.

It is religion.

The Christian Faith is the very thing that should wake us up to the existence of the three-headed hound of hell, and make us fall on our faces in penitent horror, but for many of us, religion is the very thing that ensnares us even further.

Maybe you're shocked by this revelation, but it's true. We use religion as our ultimate cover-up. We tell ourselves that if we are religious we *must* be serving others. If we are religious we *must* be full of humility, not pride. If we are religious we are not prejudiced. If we are religious we *must* be tolerant, kind, open-minded. Right?

Wrong.

In fact, too often we fall into the trap of asserting our power by using religion to control others. With endless rules and regulations and a hefty dose of guilt we manipulate and control. With "scholastic" debates about points of doctrine and morality, we assert our pride and prove ourselves not only right but righteous. We use religion to bolster our prejudices rather than challenge them. Furthermore, we do all this believing that God Himself approves. He must approve of us because we are so good. We are so right and so righteous. We are so devout and pious. We have Cerberus under control.

But it doesn't really work.

What is the result? He growls and snaps. He paces back and forth like the caged beast that he is.

Deep unhappiness brews within. Discontent lies below, sullen and glowering. A nagging awareness haunts us. All is not well. We are restless. Our desires continue to simmer. Our need for power is frustrated. Our pride is restrained. Our prejudices are stymied. We are unhappy but we don't know why.

Sometimes we lash out in unrestrained power, pride, and prejudice, and then the seven deadlies show themselves: wrath, violence, lust, greed, sloth, gluttony, and avarice.

But more often we behave ourselves. We put Cerberus back on his leash, but the restless hound is hungry. The unhappiness gnaws on our mind and heart as a dog gnaws a bone. We are unhappy because our power is restrained, but, because we have lied to ourselves, we don't know why we are unhappy.

And the heart of our life's unhappiness bubbles and brews, simmers and stews as in a witch's cauldron—and that witch is another demon from the underworld.

5

Medusa and Her Sisters

In a pre-scientific age the underworld was the lair of monsters, but so was the sea. Like the caverns beneath the surface of the earth, the raging sea was also the realm of everything dangerous, dark, and deep. It was the home of the most terrible gods—Leviathan and the most fearsome sea dragons.

In the ancient myths, Phorcys and Ceto were two of the sea monsters who mated and brought forth a whole brood of demon beasts. The most famous of their spawn are Medusa and her sisters, Stheno and Euryale. These three witches are known as the Gorgons.

A horrible hybrid of human and reptile, the Gorgons' skin is sheathed in scales, they have bronze claws, wicked wings, and their hair is a horrible tangle of vipers. The faces of the Gorgons are terribly beautiful and beautifully terrible. Medusa is the worst of the three, and if you look upon her face and meet her fiery eyes, you will be turned to stone.

Rising from the stormy depths of the human heart, Medusa represents Resentment—the sullen beast that seduces humanity. Resentment is not simply being sore because you lost the game or because Jimmy got a bigger piece of pie than you. Throughout this chapter, I will capitalize the word "Resentment" to distinguish it from the lesser "resentment," which is only a fleeting emotion.

The Resentment I am referring to is not simply the momentary emotion of feeling angry and frustrated. It is deeper and darker than that. It is the repeated reliving of a negative emotion. It is a deep-seated cycle of anger in a person's life. It is the relentless restlessness and discontent that comes from our power, pride, and prejudice being frustrated.

Neither is Resentment simply the memory of a negative experience or emotion and the regret that accompanies that memory. Resentment is the conscious, intentional, vivid reenactment of that that negative emotion. I call it the "Resentment loop."

Every reader will recognize the Resentment loop. You have been wounded in some way. There's a grievance. You've been treated unfairly. You didn't get your way. You've been offended. Your opinions were not valued. You got kicked around. You got fired. You were rejected. You were bested in a quarrel. You got hurt.

Then the Resentment loop begins. You replay the experience over and over again in your mind. You tell yourself what you are going to say the next time you see that person. "Let him wait and see!" you think. "Next time, I'll give him a piece of my mind! Next time, I tell him what I really think. Next time, I'll say … What I should have said was …" Maybe when you're alone you even voice these conversations out loud.

You've fallen into a Resentment loop.

You were seduced by the terrible beauty of Medusa. She caught your eye, and you fell into her trap. You looked at Medusa, and you became hard-hearted and hardheaded.

She turned you into stone.

Why do we fall into the Resentment loop? We fall into that negative cycle because our exercise of power was constrained.

Our pride was wounded. Our prejudices were challenged, and we didn't get our own way. So we sulk. We pout. We have one big pity party. We wallow in Resentment, and why do we do this?

Because we enjoy it. That's how seduction works. Medusa is able to lure us into her Resentment loop because it gives us pleasure. Although Resentment is a negative emotion, the Resentment loop feels good. That's because when we're in the Resentment loop, we are asserting ourselves over our rival. We feel powerful again. In our minds we prove that we are right, and they are wrong. Our pride is fed. Our prejudices have been proven. We prevail. We are omnipotent again, and that feels good.

Very good.

In fact, the Resentment loop is like a drug. It makes us feel euphoric. It makes us feel high and mighty. So we return to the Resentment loop. We play the conversations over and over again because those inner dialogues make us feel like we're in charge. It is there that we dominate and control. It is there that we rule all things. But like all drugs, the effect is not real. It wears off, and we need to go back more frequently and take a higher dosage, and soon—just like an addict; we are enslaved.

We worship Medusa as an addict worships his drug or a pagan devotee adores his dark, demonic god. Soon our hearts and minds really are hardened like stone, and we start to live in the world of Resentment. We become obsessed with our own unhappiness, and before long we are not only obsessed. We are possessed. Resentment becomes the motivating factor in our life.

As Cerberus has three heads, there are three Gorgons. Medusa's witch sisters Stheno and Euryale represent two evils related to Resentment. They are Rivalry and Revenge. As Cerberus's three heads were interdependent and intertwined, so Medusa, Stheno, and Euryale are like another unholy trinity.

Immortal Combat

They are weird sisters hunched over the bubbling, boiling, troubling cauldron of our souls. The inner discontent of Resentment searches for a focus and finds a rival. What are we resentful about? We see the other person and desire what they have — and desire to be who they are. Rivalry bubbles up, then Rivalry feeds Resentment, and Resentment feasts on Rivalry.

When we cannot have what our rival has and be who they are, we not only resent them; we want to destroy them. We blame them. Our unhappiness is their fault. We come to believe that they are the ones who have made us miserable, and we want to get rid of them — not only to take what they have, but to eliminate them and take their place.

In other words, we want Revenge. We want to get even. They have caused our unhappiness, and we demand what we imagine is justice. Revenge loves the motto "An eye for an eye, and a tooth for a tooth." But once we have our Revenge, the rival will demand his Revenge, and so the murderous cycle of Revenge and retaliation ensues.

See these Gorgons dance around the cauldron in a hideous ceremony of seething violence and despair: Resentment, Rivalry, Revenge. Resentment, Rivalry, Revenge … in an ever-descending spiral into the frozen dark where there is nothing left but Resentment, Rivalry, and Revenge.

Like Cerberus and the Minotaur, the Gorgons are creatures of the underworld, and, therefore, creatures of the dark recesses of our own minds and hearts. They dance their gruesome *danse macabre* in the dark. Like Cerberus and the Minotaur, they not only lurk in the depths, but they defend the depths from our curiosity and attempts at conversion. By blaming others, Resentment, Rivalry, and Revenge keep us from entering our own underworld.

If the male dog Cerberus represented the *animus* — the masculine side of our ego aggression, the Gorgons represent the *anima* — the feminine form of ego aggression. Whining, complaining, blaming, and planning Revenge: these are the hags howling within the hearts of both the men and women of our fallen race.

"But stop!" you say. "Is the human heart so desperately depraved? Is this really the way we are? It does not seem so to me. We do not seem so demonic. We are not such monsters. Surely not. We are not haunted by demon witches. We are ordinary good people."

But remember, like the Minotaur and Cerberus, the Gorgons are creatures of the underworld. They do not appear on the surface. They are, by their very nature, creatures of the deep. We cannot see them because, like all demons, they are liars. The Gorgons wear disguises.

You say we are not so bad? Be assured: if the person trapped in the Resentment loop has enough power, he will most certainly exact Revenge against his rivals. If we have the power, we exercise that power, but we do so in many different subtle ways.

That is the way the world turns. This is the way it has always turned: Resentment. Rivalry. Revenge. Our omnipotence frustrated, we are driven by Resentment, Rivalry, and Revenge.

However, if we do not have the power to get our own way, the Resentment will transform. Remember: Medusa is a shape-shifter. She slips and slides. The Resentment is still there. In fact, Medusa's stony spell is more potent than ever as she assumes a different form.

It works like this: the Resentful person suffers from constant, unnamed unhappiness and searches for the cause. Because of his pride and prejudice, he cannot imagine that his unhappiness could possibly be his fault. Therefore, someone else must have caused his misery. Very often it *is* someone else, and the resentful one really may have suffered at the hands of another. But the problem is, if the resentful person is powerless, there is nothing he can do about it. In that case, the Resentment loop spins even faster and with a greater intensity.

The powerless person — cursed by Medusa — begins to imagine that his unhappiness is not caused simply by one person or one incident or even a collection of incidents. Instead, it is part of a larger pattern and a larger group of people. His problem was not caused by "that woman," but by all women. Her problem was not caused by "that rich white man," but by all rich white men. Their problem was not caused by "that Hispanic or African American or Jew or Catholic, or Muslim," but by *all* Hispanics, African Americans, Jews, Catholics, or Muslims.

Once the Resentment is directed toward a group of people, it widens out. A conspiracy mentality develops. The resentful one imagines that the group of people who caused his problem are bad people. They are deliberately causing mayhem not only in his life, but in the world generally. They must be resisted. But now that his rivals are far more powerful than ever, the resentful person is even more powerless and less able to wreak his Revenge.

Before long, this slave of Medusa finds other slaves who also wallow in their frustration, and their Resentment builds into rage. They form a group to nurse their Resentment and resist the imagined enemy group that has caused the problems. With the reinforcement of the Resentment group, Medusa's slave has more power.

The Resentment group is not satisfied with discussion and debate. They want action. They need to go to war against the enemy. They develop an identity and demand change — and all of it fueled by Resentment.

Now we can understand all the revolutionary movements down through history, as well as the "identity politics" of our day. All the angry little groups of protesters are driven by the three witches: Resentment, Rivalry, and Revenge.

It doesn't matter what identity and ideology it is. It could be Marxism, Nazism, or feminism. It could be any number of religious ideologies: fundamentalism, modernism, or traditionalism. It could be a political, sexual, or economic ideology. But whatever form it takes, the inner dynamic is the same.

Despite their noble ideals and good intentions, the activism is driven by Resentment, Rivalry, and Revenge, and it is relentless. It will not stop and cannot stop. The Resentment loop becomes a whirlwind, downward spiral.

When the resentful form into a collective mob, it is truly frightening to see. Their Resentment and rage render them irrational. There is no discussion with the slaves of Medusa. They are obsessed with their righteous crusade because it has become the source of their self-esteem. Unwilling to compromise, they are driven by an unholy energy. Like the living dead they stagger on, never stopping, never resting, always seeking Revenge.

They can never be appeased because they do not want their problem to be solved. They do not want the problem to be solved because their Resentment has become the only source of meaning in their lives.

When I say that "they can never be appeased," I do not mean you should not attempt to appease them, but even if you do, they will not be satisfied. They breathe the air of Resentment. They need Resentment as a vampire needs blood. If you appease them, if you give what they demand, they will throw it back in your face with anger and demand something else or something more.

When the slaves of Medusa attain their objectives and gain power, they invariably sabotage their success. They do not want success, for that would deprive them of their grievance and their precious Resentment. They cling to their Resentment as Gollum drools over the Ring of Power.

Then there is a turning point.

Once Resentment has become the driving force of their whole life, there is a flip in values. The Resentment is no longer viewed as negative but takes on a positive value. It is no longer sweet-sour; it is completely sweet.

The Resentment now seems good, and the resentful one views himself also as good. His cause is no longer merely a fight for equality or recognition. It has become a righteous cause, and he is a glorious warrior in the battle! If he encounters opposition, he becomes a martyr in his own eyes. He is not only good, but he is the very best of men — a righteous victim, a martyr to a cause.

The poisonous Resentment, which simmered up from the person's misery, like some kind of humiliation, and self-loathing, actually becomes the source of his triumphant new self-image. He now has a vocation, something to live for and something to die for. He dons the image of the noble soul, the crusader, the martyr for a cause like some kind of superhero costume. He even seems altruistic, doing good works and helping people. Indeed, he may help others as part of his great crusade, but his good deeds are driven by hatred, not by love.

To be sure, the hatred is covered with kind words, a gentle demeanor, and the faux victim's weak smile. But the costume and the mask are part of a complex, multilayered and extravagant lie.

Beneath the activist's seeming righteousness, the Resentment and rage still simmer. Behind the superhero's cape and mask, Medusa shelters and hides. The monster lurks below the kindly surface, but in a moment of weakness the mask slips, the facade cracks. He shocks you with a snarl instead of the usual smile. His eyes flash, and you are turned to stone.

There is one more layer of this complex web of deceit that is darker still. Like those who hide their power, pride, and prejudice under the facade of religion, so the resentful hide Medusa beneath the worthy causes of religion. They get their sweet Revenge by condemning and judging others and so make themselves superior. And what better Revenge on the rival could there be but to appear better than him? And who could possibly be more deliciously superior and magnificently righteous than the religious person busy with a worthy cause?

The religiously resentful invoke God Himself to support their deception. In their own eyes, they are good, true, and righteous in all things. They are pleasing to God. They are His chosen people. Their righteous cause is His righteous cause. Their campaign against the wicked is His campaign against the wicked. They are doing His work. They are martyrs, and everyone knows God loves martyrs best of all!

The religious resentful have mastered their Father's subtle art — they clothe their dark souls in light. They resemble their father Lucifer who presents himself as a glorious angel of light.

But he is not an angel of light.

He is Sauron and Satan, the Dark Lord, the Father of Lies, and the Father of Flies.

The resentful ones are his pawns and his spawn, his deformed children and his slaves.

They are the People of the Lie.

6

Geryon and the People of the Lie

Did you think the Gorgons were terrifying and Cerberus the three-headed hound of hell was a creature of nightmares? There is more. The pit holds a yet more terrifying beast.

Meet the Geryon.

He is a mutant giant. He transmogrifies. He takes on different forms. Geryon is the grandson of Medusa and has a hound named Orthrus, who is the brother of Cerberus. This gigantic servant of Satan is unpredictable and cunning. He is always devious in the disguises he adapts.

In one account he is a giant with three heads and one body. In another myth he has three bodies but one head. Another storyteller says Geryon has six hands or six legs and bat-like leathery wings. All of the accounts reveal him to be a shape-shifter — multiform, sneaky, slithery, and sly.

The poet Dante tells us that Geryon is the guardian of the eighth circle of hell — the land of the liars, the circle of the frauds — fakers, cheats, conmen, and hypocrites. It is worth noting that the eighth circle of hell is next to the last, and the deeper you go into Dante's *Inferno*, the more horrible the monsters you encounter and the worse the punishments, because the offenses of the sinners are more horrendous.

Immortal Combat

Dante's Geryon is a gigantic beast with the paws of a lion, the wings of a bat, a scorpion's tail, and the body of the wyvern — a two-legged dragon. But crowning all these beastly attributes is something terrible and surprising: it is the head and face of an honest man.

The monster has the face of an honest man.

As you were reading, you may have thought, "This is a dark take on humanity. Surely we are not so bad, so twisted, so perverse? Do most of us ordinary folks share in such a twisted nature? Is religion itself motivated by such dark, distorted desires? If this is so, are there any truly good people, or are we all so disfigured? Is there any honesty, or are we all not only deceiving everyone, but, most of all, deceiving ourselves?

In the second part of this book we will get down to what constitutes real goodness, truth, and beauty, but to genuinely know the enemy we must go deeper into the dark, and this means we must confront the People of the Lie.

We have already seen the power, pride, and prejudice that constitute the foundation of evil. We've studied how Resentment, Rivalry, and Revenge grow out of the first three like poisonous weeds. Now we will see how these six traits manifest themselves. They are hidden within us as the People of the Lie.

The People of the Lie are symbolized by Geryon. All of them have the face of an honest man or woman. Indeed, they often have the respectable face of a member of the establishment. The "honest" face is smiling and charming. The face has good manners. The face is courteous and polite. The face is well educated. The face is caring. The face is pious. The face is even prayerful and serene. It is not only the face of an honest man; it could be the face of a seemingly good religious man. In fact, it could be the face of the very best of religious men — the pastor, the prophet, the priest, the prelate, or the pope.

Know this: Judas himself had the face of an honest man.

The Geryon is a gigantic beast, just as the presence of the People of the Lie is gigantic. Their influence is huge. Their power is enormous, but behind the honest faces are the claws of a lion, the horrible wings and body of a Nazgul, and the deadly sting of the scorpion's tail.

The People of the Lie are very difficult to spot because, like Geryon, they are expert shape-shifters. They are chameleons —reptiles who adapt to their surroundings. They fit in. They are expert actors who adapt a costume and play a part on the world's stage.

Their true beastly nature is hard to see because they always present the "face of an honest man." The lion's paws are disguised as well-manicured human hands. Their bat wings are folded and hidden in the cut of their tailored suit, and their scorpion tail is coiled and out of sight. All you can see is the smiling face and smooth manners of an honest man.

How can you spot the Geryon—one of the tribe who are the People of the Lie? There are two ways. The first is that they are never wrong. Never. When confronted with a fault, they defend themselves and deny the problem. The less expert may argue, but it is never an argument to discover truth. It is always, rather, an argument to avoid the truth, to eliminate the criticism and prove themselves right.

However, the most accomplished of the People of the Lie do not deny and defend. They deflect. With a polite nod they listen to your criticism and respond, "Thank you for that feedback. We will certainly consider your views and weigh them along with the other opinions we have received." With great skill they have deflected your criticism, deflated your attack, and proven their superiority at the same time.

The second sign that you are dealing with People of the Lie is that they always have a sacrificial lamb. Somewhere in their life, you can be sure they have a person or a group of people who they believe are the source of all their difficulties. In a family, they even call their sacrificial lamb the "black sheep." This "difficult" member of the family is the troublemaker, the oddball, the one who doesn't fit in, the one who won't play the game, the one who rocks the boat. The Geryon always has a sacrificial lamb. The People of the Lie always blame another.

They always have their victim ready for slaughter.

The black sheep becomes the target onto whom all the Geryon's own darkness is projected. The People of the Lie deny that there is anything wrong with them. They insist it is instead the black sheep who has the problem. The black sheep is the one who needs help, and if the black sheep will not receive help he will be excluded and expelled.

M. Scott Peck was a psychiatrist who explained this distorted behavior in his book *The People of the Lie*. Peck recounted various case histories to explain how the People of the Lie function within families. The family member presented to Dr. Peck for treatment was rarely the one who needed treatment.

The other family members hid their deep soul sickness from themselves and projected their distorted problems onto the black sheep. And sure enough, their sacrificial lamb began to display problems, confirming in the family's mind that he was, *indeed*, the problem child. By projecting their problems, the People of the Lie emerged neat and clean and practically perfect in every way. They did not have a problem; the scapegoat child was the problem!

One particularly chilling story Dr. Peck recounts is about Bobby—a fifteen-year-old student who was suffering from depression. He had been a straight "B" student, a gifted athlete, and a popular member of his school. Suddenly he dropped out of sports and started to flunk out. His parents, who were an upright, hard-working, churchgoing, respectable couple, sent him to Dr. Peck.

Dr. Peck began to talk with Bobby about his relationships. Bobby said he liked his parents well enough. They provided everything for him. He had no complaints.

Dr. Peck asked how they showed their love. Bobby said they gave him stuff. They had given him a Christmas present.

When Dr. Peck asked about the present, Bobby said it was a gun.

Dr. Peck asked what kind of gun.

"Just a gun."

"Are you a hunter, Bobby? Why did they give you a gun? Was it a special gun?"

"It was my brother's gun," Bobby mumbled.

"Your brother?" Dr. Peck didn't know there was a brother. "Doesn't your brother need the gun anymore?" he asked.

"He's dead."

It turned out that Bobby's parents had given him the very gun his older brother had used to commit suicide the previous Christmas.

Shocked that these seemingly good, churchgoing folks could be so insensitive and cruel, he confronted them with what they had done.

They were indignant and couldn't see the problem.

"Doctor!" protested the uppity mom. "We sent Bobby to you so you could help him! We never imagined you would blame us for his problems!"

The father pulled out his checkbook, and, smiling with suppressed anger, said, "How much do we owe you, Doctor? We need to settle up and find someone who can really help Bobby."

Then the mother played the crybaby bully. She pulled out a hankie and started to dab at her eyes. "We're so disappointed, Doctor. I suppose we'll have to keep looking for someone who really cares. Someone who is a professional."

These are People of the Lie. They are the Geryons. They are repulsive beasts but with the "face of an honest man." They are gigantic because their power is overwhelming.

Dr. Peck points out that, like their father, the Father of Lies, they are murderers. They may not murder physically, but they kill all that is beautiful, good, and true. They kill the joyful life in others, even though they may not literally slip the knife and slit the throat.

Peck outlines various characteristics of the People of the Lie. First and foremost, they are self-deceiving. They do everything they can to avoid their own guilt and project an image of perfect respectability and goodness. They devote enormous amounts of energy to maintaining their perfect facade.

Their self-deception needs to be fed constantly, and the main way they support their self-deception is by winning the admiration of others. As they convince others of their perfect goodness, their own self-image is reinforced.

They are always aware of their outward image and will be perfectly groomed, well mannered, and courteous. However, if they happen to be in the company of those who do not have civil manners, they will quickly adopt the same outward form to fit in and be thought good. They are shape-shifters.

Because they cannot face the darkness within themselves, they project their inner Resentment and rage onto specific targets. This target may be another individual or a particular ethnic, racial, or religious group. They will always project their inner darkness with a voice of self-righteous indignation and rage.

"Those filthy immigrants!" (Or insert here any other person or group.) "Somebody needs to step in and rid this country of such scum!"

This is the ugly face of the Geryon's projection, and it is all around us. However, the truly adept shape-shifter doesn't display righteous rage. That would mar his meticulously crafted self-image. Instead he will cover the projection of his rage onto others with a facade of love, compassion, and concern. Bobby's parents saw him as the problem and unconsciously wished for his death, but, outwardly, they only ever spoke about Bobby in terms of their seeming love and concern for his welfare.

"Doctor, we're so concerned for Bobby! We hope you can help. We can't understand why he is in such a downward spiral! We love him and know he can do so much better!"

The People of the Lie use manipulation, emotional blackmail, and mental and spiritual abuse to get their way. They naturally play the victims, when in fact they are the aggressors. They'll say, "After all I've done for you, this is the thanks I get??!!" Or "We're at our wit's end! We've tried so hard to help Tammy, and she simply won't cooperate!" With convincing piety they'll say, "We have prayed so much about this decision, and we really feel Sam must be confined to that mental health unit for his own good."

No. They have not prayed. They have preyed.

They have preyed on their targeted victim. They persecute their victim to confirm their belief that the black sheep is the problem. They are not doing this for anyone's benefit but their own.

Beneath their facade of warm compassion, the People of the Lie are totally lacking in empathy. They are unable to put themselves into the shoes of their victim or any victim. Even if they don't state it openly, the People of the Lie believe those who are unfortunate have brought it on themselves and deserve their misfortune.

However, while they experience no real empathy, they are expert in feigning empathy if it is required for their external appearance. They will show concern and even weep, but when no one is looking they will stop pretending.

Finally, the People of the Lie are impervious to criticism. They never apologize. They never repent. They can never be sorry because they are always and forever right and never wrong. Just as they deflect criticism by seeming to accept it, so the People of the Lie avoid saying "sorry" by pretending to apologize. They are experts of the fake apology. They will say, "I'm so sorry you were offended!" And more often than not, they will avoid apologizing by blaming others. Their failure cannot be their fault. Others must always be to blame.

The People of the Lie are the truly evil ones. They are the giant monster Geryon. They are the offspring of Cerberus and are totally enslaved to their power, pride, and prejudice. They are the sisters of Medusa because Resentment boils beneath their phony, stony facade like lava within a dormant volcano.

And they are everywhere.

The People of the Lie are all around us. They occupy the top jobs. They are the pillars of the church and state. The People of the Lie are the smooth, successful ones—the media manipulators, the polite politicians, the urbane bankers, and the smiling socialites. They are the pastors with pleasant faces, the bishops and cardinals with slick diocesan systems, and the smooth prelates in scarlet robes.

The People of the Lie have given themselves to Satan. The nightmare of demon possession as portrayed in film is terrifying and obscene, but it is also rare. Much more common is the perfect possession of the human soul by the demon Geryon. These possessed ones do not vomit and growl, levitate, spit nails, and blaspheme. They do not run across the ceiling, demonstrate supernatural strength, or growl like beasts from the depths of Gehenna.

On the contrary. They are charming and sophisticated. They are suave and svelte, respectable and smooth. They are powerful and persuasive, but deep within they are the sons and daughters of perdition. Their father is the Father of Lies, and they are the People of the Lie, and there is no human cure for them.

There cannot be a cure because a cure would have to begin with an admission that there is something wrong with them, and their whole being is founded upon their conviction that they are never wrong. They will never seek a cure — indeed, they are unable to seek a cure as long as they remain blind to their sickness.

The People of the Lie reinforce their self-deception by getting other people to believe their false personas. In doing so, the People of Lie naturally gravitate to others like themselves. With almost preternatural cunning they recognize one another and come together like magnets.

They form societies, clubs, and fraternities of mutual self-interest. These tribes feed the lies and bolster their mutual deceptions. The People of the Lie are voracious for lies. They feed one another on lies, and their individual lies are immeasurably strengthened by the consolidated lies of the tribe.

When the People of the Lie operate within a family or a community, they are destructive and fearsome enough. But when their individual behaviors become group behavior, the complexity of the lies and the labyrinthine layers of deception become a tangled net of insidious intent.

Immortal Combat

Then there is not one Geryon, but a mob of Geryons. The People of the Lie form the Tribe of the Lie, and like the living dead catching the scent of blood, the mob sets out to murder and devour.

7

Murder and the Mob

In his nightmare journey through the Inferno, the poet Dante and his guide meet the Geryon as they stand at the edge of the huge pit which is the eighth circle of hell. The gigantic beast wings its way up from the pit. They clamber onto his back, and he descends into the gaping cavity of tortured souls, like a vast strip mine with ten circular ditches, each one imprisoning a different category of deceivers and self-deceived.

The geography of Dante's hell is fascinating because the deeper you go into hell, the more serious the crimes. Most people who read the masterpiece are surprised to find the crimes they thought the worst — the sins of the flesh — at the upper levels. The ninth and deepest circle is reserved for Judas alone, but the eighth is the huge pit to which Dante consigns the People of the Lie.

This is because the more we lie, the more we have to lie to cover up the previous lies. The more we lie, the more we deceive ourselves. The more we lie, the more we are trapped in a world of deception and deceit. The more we lie the more we become like our father — the Prince of the People of the Lie.

Dante paints an accurate and grim landscape of liars with ten categories — ten tribes of deceivers. Here are the pimps, pornographers, and seducers who lie about sex — dressing up corruption as something delightful. Here flatterers are immersed in sewage as punishment for their pleasing, self-serving lies. Here are the preachers who raked in money by promulgating false religion. Imprisoned here are the New Age phonies, fakes, frauds, conmen, and counterfeiters.

All these are liars, cheats, and deceivers, but in the lowest ditches of the eighth circle are the People of the Lie — those who not only deceived others, but the self-righteous who, first and foremost, have deceived themselves. Here are the thieves — not those who steal out of greed, but those who steal because they believe another's possessions should belong to them. These are the thieves who steal not to survive or simply to take another's possessions, but those who steal the identity and life of their neighbor.

Here are the self-righteous deceivers who give bad advice to others, convincing themselves that it is good advice. Here are the self-righteous schismatics — those who form their own churches and sects, believing themselves to be better than others. Here also are the hypocrites. Doomed to wear golden robes lined with lead, they stagger under the weight of their rich robes, eternally convinced of their goodness and forever wondering what they have done to deserve such punishment.

The eighth circle is full of tortured souls who, for all eternity, continue believing in their own goodness and protesting their innocence. The eighth circle is crowded with a multitude of self-righteous liars. The pits are bulging and overflowing with the wretches. They are crammed with souls who are forever crying out, "But we were good people! We were not as bad as all that! Why are we here?" Hell is crowded with souls who believed so firmly in their own lies that they could not see they were lying.

They lied so much that they became infused and saturated with lies. They became the lie. They are the People of the Lie.

You might protest, "I see your point. They are, indeed, "The People of the Lie," Yes, they are evil, but they are rare. Most people are not like that!"

You are wrong. The perceptions and behaviors of the People of the Lie are basic to our humanity. This is the Sin of the World. This is the way of the world. This is the way we are wired. Without the grace that opens our eyes, we are all the People of the Lie. It is the default setting, and the fact that we cannot see this truth proves the point. Denying that we are the People of the Lie, in fact, proves we are members of that very horde of hypocrites.

To understand the depth of the depravity of the People of the Lie, we must study their behavior with the shrewd eye of the wise philosopher René Girard. He explains how the lie germinates in the human heart, then grows into a wild and wicked weed, spreading its shoots and vines like tentacles into every aspect of our human society.

We must remember Cerberus and the three heads of power, pride, and prejudice that are the result of the sin in the garden. When our pride and desire for power are frustrated, the monster Medusa materializes like an obscene ghoul along with her witch sisters Rivalry and Revenge.

When we do not get what our rival has, and when we cannot become who our rival is, we blame him for the problem. It is his fault. It cannot be our fault because we are right. We are good. If there is a problem, someone else *must* have caused it. Our rival is the problem, and we must find a final solution.

When this behavior expands from the individual to the tribe, it becomes even more complex. Not able to stand anyone who is "wrong," the individual joins others who agree with him. They form a tribe. They build a little fortress — a cult, a political party, a religious sect, an activist group. Safe in their little fortress, they huddle together and talk about all those people outside who are wrong, wrong, wrong. That makes the members of the tribe feel even better and stronger.

The members of the tribe feed the blaming and projection instinct in one another. They begin to think as a group. Rational thought disintegrates. Individual discernment disappears. Criticism and even the idea that criticism is possible evaporates. Groupthink burgeons like an obscene cancer or a hideous, infectious disease. The Resentment, Rivalry, and need for Revenge become the obsession of the gang.

To understand how this evil dynamic works, let us imagine there is a crisis in the tribe. It could be internal quarreling and conflict. It could be an external crisis like a famine, plague, flood, or the shadowy threat of invasion, war, or some feared but unknown disaster. Whatever the crisis, the members of the tribe seek a solution. As the problem worsens they become desperate to find relief, but to find the solution they must first identify the cause of the problem.

They cannot possibly be the cause of the problem because they are right. They are good. It is impossible that it could be their fault. The default settings of pride and prejudice have already determined that. Therefore, since the problem cannot be caused by one of the members of the tribe, it must be someone from outside the tribe.

The obvious targets are the members of another tribe. They are the rivals. They are the ones who must have caused the problem, and because the other tribe is also operating according to the same dynamic of pride and prejudice, it is very possible that the other tribe is, indeed, the cause of the crisis.

The result is a thing called "war." Seeking a solution to their crises, the two tribes blame one another. They bow down and feed Medusa and her witch sisters Rivalry and Revenge. Then they plummet into the endless, downward spiral of Resentment, Revenge, and retaliation, and the blood they shed in their endless feud is like an offering to the horrible hags from hell—the Gorgons.

Notice also the effect of war on the tribe. It unifies and excites them. War seems to solve the problem. Attacking the enemy bonds the tribe into a band of brothers. If you have any doubt, think of how many politicians, when faced with national strife, division, and crisis, start a war. Suddenly the nation is united, the flag wavers congregate, the war whoop is heard, the weapons are loaded, the boys march off to battle, and the other tribe is attacked.

However, the crisis is not always caused by the other tribe. Crises arise even when there is no other tribe. Within the tribe itself, there are constant tensions and conflicts caused by power struggles, pride, prejudice, Rivalry, and Resentment. When an internal crisis begins, the members of the tribe try to ignore it, hoping the conflict will go away. They also ignore it because they do not want to own the crisis. It can't be their problem because they are right. Their tribe is the right tribe. They are good and righteous.

The members of the tribe, therefore, instinctively blame the outsider. But if there is no outside cause, they look for the "problem" from within their own tribe. The "problem" will invariably be someone among their number who doesn't fit in—someone who is peculiar, physically disabled, or strange.

The "black sheep" may be physically disabled, mentally ill, or more stupid than the others. He may, however, be smarter, more talented, stronger, or more beautiful than everyone else. He may be different in a variety of ways. That doesn't matter. It doesn't matter how he is different. What matters is that he is different. The black sheep does not fit in, and this threatens the unity of the tribe.

The nail that sticks out must be hammered down.

Once the cause of the crisis is identified, the members of the tribe come together. Their fear and rage coalesce mysteriously and projected onto the person of blame.

First, there is gossip, but the gossip soon spirals out of control. The black sheep becomes evil in their eyes, and all manner of evil is attributed to him. The darkest Resentment and fear of the tribe boils up in hatred. Soon the "cause of the problem" is thought to be guilty of the foulest crimes, and if there is no proof of the crimes, the members of the tribe are certain this only goes to show how clever the accused is of covering up his wickedness.

Now a witch hunt atmosphere develops. The accused are suspected of being demon possessed. The black sheep are not given the right of remaining innocent until proven guilty. In the eyes of the People of the Lie, they do not need to be proven guilty. Their guilt is obvious to all. Furthermore, if anyone stands up for the accused, that person will instantly be suspected of collusion and become one of the enemies.

Fear spreads throughout the tribe. The crisis intensifies. Now *anyone* who criticizes the behavior of the tribe is part of the problem. They are clearly in league with the accused, and they, too, must be condemned. Members of the tribe now realize that the only thing worse than the accused and his defenders are the people who seem to be members of the tribe but are really one of the enemies. They are a fifth column. There is a group of traitors in their midst. They must be discovered. An inquisition must take place. All those suspected of being part of the problem in any way must be included in the purge.

Eventually the crisis will reach a climax. The accused will first be mocked, then marginalized, then excluded from the tribe. The final charge is that they are demon possessed. They are devils incarnate. They will be forcibly expelled, excommunicated, and exorcised—cast out into the outer darkness they deserve.

But of course, this does not solve the problem. As long as the expelled members remain alive, the problem remains. The accused are still present, even if they have been excluded. They lurk on the fringes. Now they are haunting the tribe by their malevolent presence. Even if they seem to submit to the tyranny of the tribe, their continued presence is a threat and an accusation.

The tribe concludes that there is only one thing to be done. The problem must be solved. There must be a final solution.

There must be blood.

So the accused are taken outside the town and killed. The killing must be violent because that is what the terrible "cause of the problem" deserves. The killing must also be public so everyone can see that the cause of the problem has been eliminated. All must see that the devil in their midst has been cast out, the troublemaker has been dealt with. The death must be horrific to act as a deterrent.

After the execution, the members of the tribe feel enormous relief. The crisis is over! Order is restored! The problem has been solved! The murderous mob is at peace. With the killing, the members of the tribe feel like their goodness and power have returned. They are once again in charge. They must be wise and good for they have eliminated the problem. In fact, they have solved the problem with a kind of magic. Their new power is like a drug. Their final solution has not only solved their problem; it has brought their people unexpected peace and bliss. Therefore, they are not only good; they are like gods with their newfound power.

The serpent was right! They *did* become like God! The realization of their great power causes them to rejoice. They dance and sing. They feast and celebrate. They worship the gods who granted them such power!

This is the way the world turns. This is the cycle of the People of the Lie. This is the Sin of the World. This is what we do.

Do you protest? "But we are not primitive tribal people!" you cry. "We do not kill our brothers! We do not lynch people anymore! We do not take victims outside the town and burn them at the stake! We do not hunt witches. We do not line people up to be beheaded!"

Have you forgotten your history? This is precisely what our human race has been doing in every age and in every corner of the globe, and recent history magnifies the fact. The twentieth century, with the ovens of Auschwitz, the long march of the Armenians, the starvation of the Ukrainians, Mao's revolution, the Gulag, and the killing fields of Cambodia and Rwanda prove the point.

Still, you say, "But *we* don't do this! We're nice people. We are not Communist killers and Nazi overlords! We defeated them!"

Stop. Look. Listen. We do this all the time. We shift the blame. We find the black sheep. We choose the victim. To be sure, we do it on a lesser scale, but we do it as individuals. We do it as families. We do it as businesses. We do it in the military. We do it as nations. We do it as political parties. We do it as racial groups. We do it as schools. We do it in religion. In fact, religious people are especially good at it. We do it in Bible study groups. We do it in parishes, churches, and religious communities. We do it all the time. We do it automatically.

We may not burn witches at the stake or wheel out the guillotine, loosen the noose or open the gas chamber door, but the same dynamic is at work when we blame others, gossip about them, mock, marginalize, and exclude them. The same ugly gods of pride, prejudice, Rivalry, Resentment, and Revenge are at work when we vilify others, destroy their reputation, and gather in elitist tribes to blame outsiders.

And are we so innocent of shedding the blood of those we blame? Violence simmers in our streets and our homes as it does in our hearts. The domestic violence and abuse continue. The vitriolic Revenge and blame displayed in divorce courts breaks lives, destroys hearts, and hurts children. The gang violence in our cities is our form of tribal violence.

Going to war to control our "vital economic interests" is tribal violence born of Rivalry, Resentment, and Revenge. Through abortion we sacrifice the lives of the innocent who stand in the way of our pride and prosperity. Euthanasia is our way of eliminating "the problem" in the same way as the commandant of Auschwitz operating the gas chambers or the tribal chieftain beheading and skinning the victim from the neighboring tribe.

Not only have we done this down through the ages, but we do it still. Furthermore, to top it all, we believe ourselves good for doing so. We believe we have come up with the final solution and that God Himself must be smiling on us. It must be that He will bless us for so brilliantly solving the problem. If you do not believe me, consider our sanctimonious war mongers, the false piety and compassion of those who promote abortion and euthanasia, and the indignant self-righteousness of those who blame the immigrants, the Jews, the liberals, the conservatives, or anyone but themselves for their problems and the problems of the world.

And here is the ultimate lie—the granddaddy of them all: we not only believe ourselves to be good for initiating the final solution of slaughter; we believe that God, too, is pleased with us. Since the killing of this victim has restored our peace and solved the problem, we think God Himself now blesses us. Therefore, to receive more of His blessings, prosperity, and peace, we believe that we must repeat this action. If the killing solved the problem, then we must kill more often—not only to solve problems, but to prevent the problems and to merit more of God's blessings.

And so in our self-righteousness and pride we turn our darkest dynamic of lies into our own little religion, and in so doing we believe that our Heavenly Father is pleased with us.

But we are mistaken.

It is not our Eternal Father who is pleased with us.

It is our infernal father. Our real father.

The Father of Lies.

8

Sacrifice and Scapegoats

In Dante's masterpiece of theological poetry, at the very bottom of the pit of hell, just below the eighth circle of the liars, frauds, and hypocrites is the vast frozen lake called Cocytus.

There, Satan himself, as a gigantic beast, is encased waist deep in ice. Like another unholy trinity, Satan has three faces: one blood red, the second a sickly yellow, and the third black. Satan's three faces mean many things, but for us they are reminders of the interwoven cords of Power, Pride, and Prejudice, interlaced with the ropes of Resentment, Rivalry, and Revenge.

These are the twisted energies that drive the Father of Lies and with which he binds his slaves. The People of the Lie have pursued their distorted paradigm of power from the beginning. Cain saw his brother Abel as his rival. He envied him, blamed him, then took him out into the field to enact the final solution—he killed his brother. Not only did Cain kill Abel, but he did not think he had done wrong. When God asked where Abel was, with adolescent insouciance Cain stuck out his chin and sassed, "Am I my brother's keeper?"

So from the beginning, Satan established this perverted pattern among his kidnapped children. The People of the Lie continued to stride down the path of power, pride, and prejudice,

Rivalry, Resentment, and Revenge. They blamed others for their own frustration and fear, and, seeking a solution, they mocked, persecuted, excluded, and finally killed the ones they perceived as the problem.

In the blindness of pride, they could never see that they were, in fact, the problem. Rivalry amongst themselves, simmering Resentment, blaming others, and the threat of Revenge contaminated their communities like a noxious contagion. Their crises were within — within their own families, their own communities, and within their own darkened hearts.

To avoid plummeting into bloody chaos, they instinctively directed their nameless fears and simmering rage toward a scapegoat, and by eliminating that target, a pressure valve was opened. Through the murder of the victim, the rage was released. For a moment, there was resolution and peace. The problem was solved, and in their sudden surge of joy they celebrated with a feast.

Released from their crisis, the tribe of liars felt exhilarated and exonerated. Then, when the next crisis arose, they knew what to do. They remembered how the problem was solved before. Instinctively, they searched for the cause of the new problem. Another victim was discovered, blamed, marginalized, persecuted, excluded, and finally lynched, stoned, hung, gutted, burned, or beheaded.

With this killing, the People of the Lie felt the same thrill. Once more, they felt resolution and peace. Once more, they feasted. Once more, they felt the approval of the gods. Once more, they felt the godlike surge of power. And like every addict, they came to realize that to get the high they needed to repeat the process, they would have to do this every week and every day. So the murder of the scapegoat became a routine and a ritual.

The peace and power they felt after the murder was mysterious. Why did this solution feel so right and so good? How did it work? They concluded that the gods — so fickle and capricious — must have blessed them. The gods must have been pleased with the sacrifice. That is why they blessed the tribe with prosperity, peace, and power.

So the killing became not only a ritual, but a religion. It became an intricate system of sacrifice, complete with a hierarchy and hierophants, myths, mysticism, and metaphysics. For the sacrifice to have its desired effect, rules were established to choose the correct victim. Only priests could perform the sacrifice, and strict rubrics determined exactly how the sacrifice was to be offered.

This sick satanic system is everywhere in human history. From Aztecs to Aborigines and from Native Americans to Neanderthals, the scapegoats were found, and the ritual sacrifices were made. Druids and Germans, Mayans and Etruscans, Persians and Polynesians — all these various cultures made their sacrifices to the gods.

The Father of Lies, a murderer from the beginning, established lies and murder as the cornerstone of his kingdom. Wherever human society was found, the People of the Lie flourished through their systems of sacrifice. Furthermore, they concluded not only that the gods wanted them to do this, but that the gods *required* them to do this. If another crisis arose, they believed it must mean the gods were displeased, and more sacrifices would be required.

And they continued to believe their own sick logic. The religions of the lie became society's default setting. Bound in bloodshed and wrapped in an unbreakable web of lies, the sons of Cain were in bondage to the ancient Murderer. The whole world belonged to him, his demonic minions, and his human slaves.

This is the Sin of the World. It is the dark energy force that motivates the bitter heart of man. Not only is this twisted system of persecution, exclusion, and murder at the heart of human behavior, but we are blind to it. Because of pride and prejudice we honestly believe we are doing God's will by rooting out the "problem" and eliminating it, and if anyone suggests otherwise we will attack them with the utmost vehemence.

Do you imagine that this Sin of the World only operated among the ancient Aztecs, the Iroquois, the Canaanites, or the Celts?

You are wrong. It is right under our noses. It operates in ordinary families in suburban America. Nice families. Families who go to church.

I once had to counsel an outwardly good, churchgoing family with three children. They had chosen their bright and talented but eccentric daughter—we'll call her Carrie—as the black sheep. Carrie's unusual behavior attracted the negative attentions of the whole family. Everything she did was wrong, and the family members' criticism of her was relentless.

As is so often the case, the family's persecution of Carrie made the situation worse. She began to behave badly, and this only confirmed their assertion that she was "difficult." The more they victimized her, the more her behavior deteriorated until she was acting out the role completely. She became the rebel, the bad girl, the one who they suspected was taking drugs and sleeping with her boyfriend.

They planned an intervention in which Carrie would be abducted and taken to a reform school. At that point, I asked to see the rest of the family together. When I suggested that they were part of the problem, the whole family—who were normally the politest Christian people—exploded in unholy rage. Suddenly their smiles turned to snarls. It was like demons had been exposed. The father rose up in self-righteous anger and asked me to leave.

I never saw the family again, but I stayed in touch with Carrie and watched as she was eventually expelled from the family and cast out to survive on her own. She survived, but her life was a disaster of loneliness and poor choices.

Did they murder Carrie? Not literally, but they certainly killed the abundant life within her. They may not have killed her physically, but they most certainly ruined her life, and is that so very different?

When Jesus Christ talks about "things hidden from the foundation of the world," this is the mystery to which He is referring. The entire worldly edifice is founded on lies, and the insidious truth about the People of the Lie is that they will do everything they can to protect and perpetuate the lie. They interweave more lies with the first lies until the entire system is a vast network of smoke and mirrors, costumes, masks, and facades—a huge web of interlocking and interdependent lies.

The system of lies has a negative energy force of its own. It is like a pit of vipers, writhing and coiling, always planning to strike. Eventually the dynamic of lies reaches a climax. The dark cauldron boils over, and violence erupts. And the system of sacrifice is the way the society of lies channels the violence.

This ancient system of sacrifice was the foundation of human society in ancient times. It developed so that the sacrifice became not only the way to appease the gods, but also a way to seal a peace treaty between warring tribes. To end the cycle of Revenge and retribution, the chiefs from both tribes would offer their son or daughter or a young warrior or virgin from their tribe as a peace offering. The child would die instead of the people.

The war would cease, and the covenant was sealed in the blood of the sacrifice.

The sacrifice also became the way to establish peace with the ancestors. So the souls of the dead would not haunt or curse the living, a sacrifice was offered to appease them. The sacrificial system was an integral part of the worldview. It was the blood that kept society alive. Thus it had been from the beginning. Everyone understood it. It was the way the world was wired.

In some civilizations, such as the Aztecs', the ritual was highly developed, and thousands of victims were slaughtered. In some places the victim was a defective, a foreigner, a beggar, or a madman. In other places they offered their children, their young virgins or handsome warriors. Sometimes the king or members of the royal family would be slain. In other places they stepped away from human slaughter and substituted animals.

Notice how monolithic and overwhelming this lie became. It was impossible to break the system. If you tried to unmask the liar and reveal the cruelty and unfairness of the bloodshed, you would become the next victim of the mob.

The victim process was not only the foundation of society —like all religions, it was interwoven into everything. How could anyone hope to untangle a lie that was knitted into every aspect of life? In ancient societies everyone from the king to the priests, shamans, seers, and ordinary people were involved in the daily, demonic system of murder.

It was their worldview, their belief system. It was their art, their science, their politics, and their economics. It was a tower of terror, an impregnable prison, a steel fortress. It was absolute. Monolithic. Total. Satan had it locked down. It was unbreakable.

Nevertheless, God had a plan, and it began with one man. That man was Abraham, and through him God would plant a seed of light within death's dark kingdom. First, he promised Abraham a great family. His family would be the one to break the dominion of death and bring life to the world. Then he blessed Abraham and his wife with a son named Isaac, which means "laughter," because Isaac would be the beginning of God's great joke.

Then God took the first step in His secret plan to undermine Satan's stranglehold. He gave Abraham an incredibly cruel command. He told him to take his son up to the holy mountain Moriah and slit his throat. Isaac was one of the elect—elected to be killed, that is. Why did God command this, and why did Abraham obey?

Preachers often say, "God was testing Abraham's faith." What kind of a god does something like that? Does a loving father test his child's trust in him by telling the child to go play in the middle of the highway? I don't think so. The "test of faith" was something more profound than simply, "Go ahead and do this, but don't worry; I'll bail you out at the last minute." The test of faith was Abraham's participation in God's plan to overcome Satan and regain control of the silent planet.

And why did Abraham obey God so faithfully? It must have been because the practice of sacrificing one's children was part of his culture. To slit the throat of your own son was not so unusual. That's what people did to appease their gods. God's request was, therefore, in line with Abraham's cultural expectations, and so Abraham was not surprised by the command.

What *did* surprise Abraham was God later telling him that he did not have to sacrifice his son after all. For the first time since Cain killed Abel, God whispered to humanity that human sacrifice was *not* necessary. God Himself would supply the sacrifice. There was a ram in the thorny thicket, and the ram was the answer.

An animal could be substituted for the son.

This new kind of sacrificial offering was solidified further when Abraham's descendants were slaves in Egypt. The angel of death passed over the homes in the land, bringing death to the eldest son of every family. But Abraham's descendants were commanded to kill an innocent lamb instead. The lamb was the answer.

An animal could be substituted for the son, and they called that Passover lamb "the Lamb of God."

With that, an alternative was established, and from then on Abraham's descendants continued that system of sacrifice with some important differences from the rest of the Satan-dominated world around them.

The sacrifice of the chosen people would bring pardon and peace through the blessing of God — not the curse of Satan. Moses established for the Hebrew people a system of sacrifice whereby grain and wine were offered or animals were slaughtered and burned on the altar. The offerings were made in reparation for sin, to offer thanks, and seek forgiveness.

In addition to these offerings, there was another that was yet more mysterious. On the Day of Atonement, two goats were to be taken to the temple. One would be killed as a sin offering. The priest took the second and laid his hands on its head, symbolically transmitting the sins of the people. Then the animal — literally, the scapegoat — would be taken out into the wilderness and either left to the wild beasts or pushed over a cliff. And so the sins of the people were transferred and obliterated.

In the pagan systems of sacrifice, the victims were killed simply to appease the gods. The pagan peoples were blind to the dark dynamic of power, pride, Resentment, Rivalry, and Revenge. They made their sacrifices in primitive ignorance, torturing and shedding blood in a haze of superstition and fear.

The Hebrew system was different. They understood that the Satanic system was founded on pride and motivated by Rivalry, Resentment, and Revenge. They understood the difference between the perverse power of projection and the mysterious transfer of sin to the sacrificial scapegoat.

While still bound to the practice of sacrifice, they broke the Satanic system from the inside out. They broke the power of Rivalry through reparation, broke Resentment through reconciliation, and broke Revenge through forgiveness.

The Hebrew system was the secret start of God's plan to break man's bondage to Satan, but it wasn't enough. The dark sin of Cain who killed his brother and the whole network of evil that grew from the first murder still had to be broken forever.

But how could it be broken? Those who were locked in bondage to this Sin of the World didn't even know they were in bondage. They thought what they were doing was good and pleasing to God.

Despite the glimmers of light in the Hebrew religion, mankind remained in chains, and Satan's hold on his dread kingdom seemed absolute.

Where was the warrior who could defeat the dragon? Where was the one who would engage him in battle? Where was the Prince of Light who could vanquish the Dark Lord?

An open attack would most certainly fail. How can you set free prisoners who do not know they are in chains? How can you heal those who do not believe they are diseased? How can you liberate slaves who mistake their slavery for security? Not only was the whole human race enslaved to Satan, but every prophet, philosopher, seer, or saint who tried to reveal their slavery and lead them to the light was thrown into the pit, persecuted, tortured, and killed.

Immortal Combat

God could only break the power of Satan with a secret plan. Cain's brother Abel would rise. There would be a second Adam, and He would infiltrate this world with such secret humility that Satan in his pride would miss it. Another Son, a second Isaac, would sneak into the dragon's dark domain and defeat it from within.

Part 2

The Sword of Light

9

The Secret Son

There is a plot line so well loved and well worn that storytellers can't resist falling back on it time and again. I don't know if it has a name, but it could be called "The Triumph of the Secret Son."

The story is simple: There is an evil power that dominates the world. Hidden deep within that world is a secret son. He is an orphan boy, tucked out of sight with a humble working family. He is of mysterious parentage and has a secret destiny, but he grows up in safety in the most ordinary and humble of homes.

He is the one destined to defeat the overwhelming evil. His mission is to discover and then fulfill that destiny. His humility will be his secret weapon. His insignificance will be his shield. His weakness will be his strength.

Eventually his quest will bring him to the threshold of the domain of the evil power. Once there, he pushes on to penetrate the heart of darkness, and he prevails through feats of courage and cleverness. Finally, he fights the Dark Lord face-to-face in a duel unto death. In that battle he sacrifices everything to destroy his nemesis once and for all. Having conquered, the orphan hero returns as the triumphant but wounded warrior.

Yes, it is the orphan Luke Skywalker, residing on his uncle's farm on the planet Tatooine. It is Clark Kent, taken in by

Jonathan and Martha in Kansas. It the lonely Frodo Baggins, adopted by his uncle Bilbo. It is Peter Parker, living with Uncle Ben and Aunt May. It is Indiana Jones, searching for his father; Dr. Neville of *I Am Legend*, separated from his wife and child; Neo of *The Matrix* alone in his room; and Dorothy, traveling to Oz to find her way home.

It is Hercules, Theseus, Orpheus, and any number of other solitary heroes who play out the part of the secret son. The details, the cultures, and the settings change, but the storyline remains the same.

Why does the secret superhero story echo down from the ancient myths to modern movies? Because it is the true story of mankind's liberation from the kingdom of death and darkness, which I described in the first half of this book.

This timeless story is *the* story which explains everything. Looking forward and looking back, all the stories point to the great story—that great story that tells us who Jesus Christ really is.

He is the Secret Son.

One of the most tiresome aspects of being a Christian is having to push through the crowd of phony Jesuses. All the theologians, Gospel scholars, writers, and historians who attempt to paint a portrait of the historical Jesus only end up painting a portrait of themselves with long hair, a beard, and a halo. The filmmakers, playwrights, novelists, and producers of Broadway musicals also do no more than remake Jesus in their own image. This Jesus is a kind of magic mirror. If we are ego bound we look at him and see ourselves.

All the fake Jesuses look like what we think Jesus might have been, but when you poke them they whistle, wheeze, and zoom about the room like a punctured balloon. When you look closely, you realize the phony Jesus is a mirage. It is a counterfeit.

The real Jesus remains a mystery.

Is He the rebellious hippie of *Jesus Christ Superstar* and *Godspell*? Is He a political activist intent on overthrowing the Romans or a pacifist peacemaker? Is He a mystic who retreats to His mountain cave to pray, or is He a charismatic evangelist who heals people and casts out demons? Is He a profound and learned rabbi or a self-taught country preacher? Is He a macho prophet with a whip who overturns the tables or a sissy who blesses children and preaches to the birdies and flowers? Is He a clever debater who knows exactly what He's doing or a naive country bumpkin who is out of His depth? Is He a martyr for His cause or a simple rube who gets caught up in events too complex for Him to comprehend?

The problem with all the Jesus portraits is that the scholars and pundits who have proposed the portraits focus on what Jesus *did* rather than who He was. Think about this: if you are trying to understand a person of your acquaintance, you soon realize that you will never really know him or her if you only focus on their words and actions. It is easy to make an assessment of the person according to what they do or say, but what they do or say is not who they are.

Their words and actions may be the outer workings of who they are, but who they are is much bigger and more complex than simply what they do and say. To understand who they are, you must explore their origins and their destiny—where they came from and where they are going.

To understand a person fully we must understand not only how he lives, but what he lives for. More importantly, we must not only understand what they live for, but what they would die for.

This leads us to ask, "What would Jesus Christ die for?" The answer is well known: He died to take away the Sin of the World.

What is the "Sin of the World?" It is the whole insidious network of deceitfulness, darkness, despair, and death I described in the first half of this book.

Christ died to defeat death's dark kingdom, and He knew that was His destiny from the beginning. That is why he did not reject the recognition of his cousin John the Baptist, who pointed to Jesus and proclaimed in public, "Behold the Lamb of God who takes away the sins of the world!"

John and Jesus both understood. He was Isaac's substituted ram; He was the One who was to come. The Suffering Servant. The scapegoat. The Passover Lamb.

Let us be perfectly clear. Jesus was not a hippie revolutionary. He was not a sappy, fake Franciscan, preaching to birds and hugging trees. He was not a concerned social worker or an activist for the poor. He was not simply a preacher, a prophet, or a priest. Jesus was not a stern rabbi or a wild-eyed charismatic healer. He was not a rabble-rousing revolutionary, a mystical mentor, or a simple country preacher.

Jesus was the Secret Son. He came into this world to be the wounded warrior. His sole mission was to be the Lamb of God who takes away the Sin of the World.

Once we recognize Jesus as the Secret Son — the one who comes as God's secret agent in this world — everything else makes sense. Try to grasp this: Jesus came into the dominion of Satan to defeat the Prince of Darkness on his own territory. He came into this silent planet to reclaim it for His Father, the Creator. He came secretly and silently, and kept the secret silence of His mission right up until the final week of His life.

Once you realize who Jesus really is, everything in the Gospel falls into place. Why, when He healed people, did He say, "Do not tell anyone!" Why did He suddenly slip away from the crowds?

Why, when He revealed His true identity to His disciples at the Transfiguration, did He tell them to keep quiet? This puzzle, known as the Messianic Secret makes sense when we realize that Christ was the Secret Agent—the Secret Son. Rather than it being a curious puzzle for the scholars to solve, the Messianic Secret becomes the key to everything else.

Why did Christ teach in parables and speak in riddles? Why did He preach the coming of the kingdom of God but draw back from the realization of that kingdom? Why did He fall silent when His enemies demanded that He tell them who He really was? It was because He was the Secret Son. He was the warrior from another realm who was on a secret mission. He was the Son of God disguised as a son of man.

This is the prevailing theme in the New Testament and the writings of the Fathers of the Church. This is how the first Christians understood Christ. They saw that He was the long-lost King, returning to claim His kingdom. They saw Him as the Triumphant Truth—the one who defeated the Father of Lies on his own turf.

Once we see Him as the Secret Son, the entire Gospel account shines as though we are seeing it for the first time or in a new dimension. See this Secret Agent from the other side? He was born on the run, already a renegade. He, with His mother and foster father, lived the life of a fugitive—escaping danger by fleeing to Egypt. Then, when He returned with His family, they found a hideout in Nazareth.

The archeologists tell us that Nazareth itself was no more than a simple farm hamlet: a handful of homes—the huddled housing of an extended family—farmers, builders, and craftsmen. The Secret Son was hidden in a peasant home far from the attention of worldly people. When He did appear on the scene, it was to preach in this backwater to crowds of poor people. At best, the Secret Son appeared to be no more than just another itinerant country preacher.

Then, when His fame began to grow, He kept His cover. He told those He healed not to speak of it. He told the demons who recognized him to keep quiet. He told His disciples who discerned his identity not to speak of it. Only in the last week of His life, when He was going to His final battle, did He begin to declare openly who He really was. By then, the Secret Son, the man of mystery, continued to mystify both His followers and His enemies.

Therefore, if you want to understand how God planned to overcome the Sin of the World, you must understand that, from the Fall of our first parents, He had this plan in mind.

A second Adam would slip into this world. A second Abel would come to seek and to save His murderous brother Cain. A second Isaac would come to bear the wood of sacrifice up the mountain of Moriah. A second Joseph, thought long dead, would rise to save His brothers from death. This secret had been hidden from the foundation of the world. It was the secret hidden in the Passover lamb, the scapegoat, the sins and repentance of David, and the pains of the Suffering Servant.

The Secret Son's simple and overwhelming weapon was His ordinary humanity and His hidden divinity. Although He was God, He did not consider divinity as something to be claimed and proclaimed, but He took the form of a slave.

He was small. He was unassuming. He seemed to be a nobody. He was just a builder and a part-time country preacher. He seemed like a hick from the sticks. He worked with His hands and probably spoke with a hillbilly accent. In this humble carpenter, the Creator Himself was hidden.

What a man! What a plan!

The story of the Secret Son was not simply God's eternal plan; it is His only plan. This is the way He always works. We love all that is splashy and flashy. We like successful campaigns and slick public relations. We like the razzle-dazzle of celebrities, fame, and fortune. Not God. All the famous people in His kingdom began in secret. Their marvelous accomplishments in the Faith began in secret. Therefore, if we want to reach the kingdom of God, we will do all our works in secret. We will start by going into the hidden places of the heart. Our life will be hidden with Christ in God.

To engage in the battle, we will not trumpet our plans or complain about the evil in the world or the Church. We will not organize activists, publish papers, or plan a great campaign. To start, we will roll up our sleeves and do what we can with what we have, where we are.

We will go incognito. We will be princes of the kingdom disguised as paupers—God's secret agents in the world. This is how we will fit into His battle plan.

At the center of this eternal plan was a secret intervention that involved one person who is above all other created beings. It was not a magnificent angel, a Herculean hero, or a glorious gladiator.

It was a little girl.

10

The Little Lady

There is a scene in the film adaptation of *Lord of the Rings* for which I would happily watch the whole three part, extended, nine hours' worth of movie.

The city of Gondor is besieged by the allied armies of the Dark Lord, Sauron. All seems hopeless, but the riders of Rohan arrive at the final hour. They sweep onto the plain of battle and engage the enemy. In the midst of the battle, the Nazgûl — the witch-kings of Mordor — on their terrible winged lizards, swoop down and pluck up the riders and their horses in their talons.

Disguised among the horsemen is Eowyn, the princess of Rohan. In the heat of battle she is unhorsed. Theoden, her king, has fallen beneath his steed and one of the Nazgûl steps down from his fearsome flying dragon to devour Theoden and scatter the riders of Rohan.

Eowyn stands up in her armor, draws her sword, and defies the Nazgûl. He snarls in his pride, "You fool! No man can kill me!"

At that, the little lady sweeps off her helmet. She tosses her head, her gloriously golden hair shakes free, and she declares, "I am no man!" Then she plunges home her sword, slays the witch-king, and severs the head of the dragon.

Immortal Combat

It is a perfect re-telling of the eternal plan. The woman fell first into the enemy's trap, but once ensnared, it was the woman who would set in motion the Dark Lord's defeat.

If the Father wanted to invade Satan's kingdom of death, the best way would be for Him to invade from the inside. So His plan was to do just that. He would begin in the smallest, most hidden way. He planned to infiltrate the silent planet in a manner that Satan would never in a million years even begin to imagine. God would use a person not only beyond suspicion, but a person the proud spirit Satan would certainly overlook. He would use a person completely hidden and insignificant—a person nobody would give a second glance.

A little girl. A little lady.

She was the one. She was the turning point. In a stroke of creative brilliance, God chose her to be the Eowyn who would trample down the dragon. She would wield the sword to penetrate the lizard's scaly skin. She did so right at the weakest point in his hide: his pride.

The Little Lady is the exact opposite of the dragon. She is the antidote to his poison. Her simple honesty counters the extravagantly complicated infrastructure of lies he spent eons constructing. She is humble in the face of his pride. She is openhearted, innocent, and free, and her childlike trust and goodness deflates the pompous arrogance of Satan the slave master.

Remember, he was the lord of the world. He had forged interwoven cords of evil to keep mankind captive. Imagine him as the master of a vast city in which each high tower is a prison house. Every street is a dark alley of depravity. Every courtyard is the scene of bloody slaughter. Every cellar is a dungeon of torture and terror. Every penthouse in every skyscraper is a banquet hall of decadence and despair.

Then imagine that this dark city has been lit with bright lights. It has been turned into Vanity Fair. The sinister towers are covered with illuminated billboards. Like Piccadilly Circus, Las Vegas, or Times Square, all is glittering, glitzy, and glamorous. The ground floor windows are filled with seductive entertainments. The restaurants are alluring and full of laughter. Amusement parks offer thrills and diversion. The theaters beckon, and the sports stadiums are thronged with cheering crowds. The dark city has been decorated with delight, and the slaves wander the streets in an eternal delusion and a never-ending search for happiness, which spirals ever downward into despair.

Push your imagination further. The facade is not all bright lights and dazzling entertainment. The dark chambers are also masked by the ivy-covered halls of the university, the Palladian parliaments of the ruling class, and the paneled libraries of the academic elite. The palaces and basilicas of bishops, the mahogany board rooms of bankers, the comforts of the country clubs, and the castles of the grandest of the grandees—all these provide the sleekest of facades beneath which the insidious forces surge.

This is the world the Dark Lord forged. It is the festering fruit of power, pride, and prejudice. It is driven relentlessly by the Resentment, Rivalry, and Revenge always churning within the heart of man.

In the midst of this comes the Little Lady. She is a virgin, but not simply because she never had sexual relations. That would be a negative definition—defining a person according to something they have never done. No. Her virginity is not defined by something she has never done, but by who she is.

She is not just a virgin—she is virginal. We say she is a virgin as a forest that has never been cut is virgin. She is fresh and free as a day in May. She is as pure as a glass of spring water in summer. She is as unconsciously perfect as a laughing child at play.

She is a virgin, but she is not a weakling. Indeed, she is as strong and determined as the fiercest warrior. She sees the battle clearly and is not confused. She may be as soft as moonlight, but she is also as hard as diamonds. She is as glittering sharp as a sword, but she is not secretive or shrewd. There is nothing untruthful about her. She is as transparent as crystal, as simple as sunlight, and as beautiful as a rose.

Stop for a moment and consider the brilliance of this plan to undermine the Dark Lord and his foul kingdom. You may remember that the bondage began with a bad choice. Eve chose the wrong chalice. She chose poorly. With that choice came the knowledge of good and evil. With that choice came the exercise of power.

Adam and Eve and all their children realized they had power. From that power came pride. Pride is the foundational assumption that *I am right*; I have made the right choice; I am my own lord because I can exercise power. The third head of Cerberus, the hound of hell, is prejudice. Power produces pride, that invulnerable and unshakeable assumption that *I alone am right* produces prejudice: I am right, and if I am right, you are wrong. Power. Pride. Prejudice. The three howling heads of the hound of hell.

Do you see the simplicity of the plan? This Little Lady from Nazareth, this pure child in innocent trust makes the choice to give up her power. She says with an open and joyful heart, "Let it be done unto me according to your Word." With that choice she relinquishes power and pulls the plug on pride and prejudice.

When the central head of Cerberus falls, the other two vanish. Pride and prejudice were interdependent and intertwined with power. When the Little Lady decapitated power, the other two slavering heads of the serpent-hound were also crushed. When power was punctured, pride and prejudice disintegrated into dust.

The brilliance of this plan was that it was done in secret. But this was not the secrecy of subterfuge and spies. This was not the secrecy of lies and deceit. This was the secrecy of simplicity. It was the hiddenness of humility. It was secret and safe because it was small.

The choice of this Little Lady took place in a farming hamlet in a backwater county of a despised province of the mighty Roman Empire. The princess of this new kingdom was a peasant. She was a Cinderella, lowly and lovely.

Why was this brilliant? Because the Dark Lord is a strutting Darth Vader. He is a ham actor, one who loves the spotlight and the adoring applause. He sees himself as a great lord of the world. He loves the processions of power, the trappings and ceremonies of grandeur. He envisions himself surrounded by a court of admiring lackeys, enthroned and served by an army of dedicated devotees.

For God to begin His rescue mission with a peasant girl? It was unthinkable.

Impossible.

Satan would never, ever in a million years imagine that the Almighty would stoop so low. He was incapable of imagining the secret plan.

The Dark Lord was the first misogynist. From the beginning, he despised these new creatures. But most of all, he despised the females. He hated the woman's beauty. He laughed at her naivety. He scorned her emotions and manipulated her desires. He used them and tossed them away, and if he hated and ignored women, he had even less time and attention for unformed, ignorant, and foolish little girls.

So God used a little girl to slip beneath the radar.

The great plan that was hidden from the foundation of the world was about to come into play. Hidden away in a hovel, the Little Lady went about her business. Secret and small. Step by step. Steady and sure. Sweet and smiling. Innocent and pure. Unsuspecting and unsuspected. She was the perfect enemy agent and a devastating warrior in the immortal combat.

From her we learn the first fundamentals of engaging in immortal combat ourselves. It is simple, but it is not easy. This fight is the work of an instant and the work of a lifetime. First, as the Little Lady did, we lay down our own power. To overcome everyday evil we must say, "Thy will, not mine be done." The first action and prayer of each day must be, "Here I am, Lord. I come to do Your will."

Without this prayer, every other prayer is nothing but empty words. But with this prayer, every other prayer and action is infused with the divine power. Every day, if we say this prayer — if we *really* say this prayer — then the other two heads of pride and prejudice will begin to shrivel and eventually vanish from our lives.

We will become who we were created to be, and that is the definition of humility. We will have genuinely open minds and generous hearts, and that will be the defeat of prejudice. Then, when these things begin to happen, we, like the Little Lady, will soon come to learn that "with God all things are possible."

Then, and only then, will we be able to don the armor and begin our participation in the immortal combat to overcome everyday evil.

The devil, that old fool, is *still*, after all these eons, a proud spirit. Even now, he cannot comprehend the possibility that you or I might really, honestly, truly, and whole heartedly be able and willing to say that simple prayer: "Here I am, Lord. I come to do Your will."

He thinks our prayers are playacting. Despite all the evidence, he cannot understand that we would yield our wills to his eternal enemy. He cannot imagine it. Despite his losses and his terrible defeat, he still underestimates the power of the Little Lady and her children.

For this Little Lady is the warrior who tramples his head; and it is her children — bearing the sky blue banner of the Immaculata — who undermine his power with her purity and who defeat his pride and prejudice with her prayer: "Thy will be done."

11

The Full, Final Sacrifice

At the beginning of this book, I asked, "What does it mean to say, 'Jesus died to save us from our sins?' How could the execution of a political prisoner two thousand years ago possibly 'wash away' the naughty things you and I have done? How does that work? How can it be that the death of a wandering preacher 'takes away the Sin of the World?'"

This chapter will give the answer, and if you slow down and read closely to really understand, what I will explain will shake you to the very core of your being. Suddenly you will see it, and you will understand not only with your head, but with your heart.

Then your heart will be broken, but that is not a bad thing. For only when your heart is broken can the good Lord enter in.

The first thing to remember is that the "naughty things we have done" (even if they are actually very wicked) are not the same thing as the Sin of the World. Those bad things we've done and the good things we have left undone are only symptoms of the real problem. They are manifestations of the sickness. They are the lesion on the skin that signals a much deeper disease.

The second thing to remember is that this sickness is hidden from us. The Sin of the World, which is within us and woven into the very fabric of this world, is like a hideous cancer that moves around within the body, always changing its appearance. This sin sickness is, by its fundamental nature, deceitful. It is a lie, through and through. It lives to deceive and loves to disguise itself.

The Sin of the World is camouflaged. Its master is a shape-shifter himself, a master of disguise and subterfuge. We can't see it, and just when we do get a glimpse of it, like a serpent it slithers away and is gone. We are, therefore, blind to the very sickness that needs to be healed.

In the first half of this book, I tried to describe the Sin of the World. The Sin of the World is a labyrinth of lies — layer upon layer of interlaced and interdependent deceptions beneath a veneer of honesty. Each layer of lies is more subtle and covered with even more sugar icing than the last. To understand what the death of Jesus really means, review again just what the Sin of the World is and how the Lord Jesus Himself was strangled and entangled in the serpent's coils.

Our first parents believed the serpent's lie and made their choice. They chose power, and so pride was established — the unquestioned assumption that *I am right*. With pride came prejudice, because, if I am right, then those who have chosen differently must be wrong.

The assumption and utter conviction that we are right clashes with the power, pride, and prejudice of others. Even though we are convinced they are wrong, we still resent what they have. We are in conflict. They become our rival, and this conflict seethes and surges in the heart. Eventually, like a dormant volcano, it spews forth. Rivalry boils over into the burning desire for Revenge.

Smeagol steals the Ring of Power. Cain slays his brother, Abel. King David kills his friend to take his wife. Horrible bloodshed enters the world. Revenge stalks the Rival, and murder lies lurking like a wolf at the door.

"But this is unpleasant!" you might say. "We do not like to think of ourselves like this! It cannot be true that we are sons and daughters of Cain! We are not Gollum! Our hearts are not filled with Resentment, Rivalry, and Revenge! We are not murderers and thieves!"

Instinctively we turn away from the darkness. We deny the truth, and the lies begin to spiral and spin, like a spider weaving a web. We quickly learn to create false images of ourselves. We create clean and tidy worlds where everything and everyone appears to be perfect. We groom our appearance. We become respectable and successful. We cultivate our good manners and make rules to live by. Our education trains us to play this game. So we keep the hound Cerberus, with his three heads of power, pride, and prejudice, muzzled and on a short leash. We imprison the Minotaur in the dungeon below the glittering palace of our outward life.

We devote huge amounts of our emotional, mental, and spiritual resources to constructing and projecting our fantasy selves. Most alarming is the fact that we often use religion as part of this enterprise. We use religion to complete the polished effect, making ourselves into the nice, clean, happy people we want to believe ourselves to be. And the more successful we are at creating this artificial, shiny, good person, the more we (and other people) believe the glittering image we have created.

We become shape-shifters—the People of the Lie. Blind to this complex and convoluted deception, all our efforts and energy are devoted to maintaining the elaborate fiction of our supposed goodness. As we create these false self-images and artificial worlds, we believe what we are doing is good. We are good people. What we are doing *must* be good!

We are clean. We are controlled. We have our lives ordered. We obey the rules. We conform to expectations. We go to church.

We do our duty. Everything is shipshape. Evil people? Surely not. People of the Lie? It cannot be. We are *good* people. In fact, we are the best.

Despite all this, there are pains and problems in our world. Things go wrong. We are not, in fact, practically perfect in every way. Things unravel. The mask slips. Unhappiness murmurs in the dark. We are restless. Something is wrong. But because we are convinced that we are the best, the problems must be someone else's fault. Seeking to solve the problem, we look for the person or group of people who must have caused it.

When that person or group has been identified, we rise up with all the other "good people" to persecute, marginalize, exclude, expel, and finally execute the person we believe has caused the problem. Once we have killed the victim, believing we have solved the problem, we celebrate.

"But I am not like that!" you cry. "We are not like that! We do not persecute and kill!

Are you sure? Every time you blame or judge another person, you participate in the Sin of the World. Whenever you gossip about others or marginalize and accuse another person, you share in the sin of Cain. Whenever you prop yourself up by putting another person down, you plunge into this dark place. Whenever you blame another group of people for your problems, or the world's problems, you reveal your Resentment, Rage, and thirst for Revenge.

"But I have not killed anyone!" you protest.

Perhaps not. But you have blamed some person or some group of people for your problems. You have wished them dead, have you not? Not literally dead, perhaps, but you have cut them off. You have refused to speak to them. You have maligned them to others. You have destroyed their reputation. You have been happy to see them suffer.

This frightening dynamic is the Sin of the World. This is the cycle of death and destruction in which the Dark Lord had enslaved the human race. This sick downward spiral is so pervasive and permanent because we are blind to it. We are chained in a cave with our back to the light. All we can see are shadows, and we believe the shadows to be reality.

How can this evil be broken? How can a cure be found if the diseased one does not believe himself to be sick? How can the system of interwoven lies be broken?

The evil system could only be broken from the inside out. Should anyone attempt to criticize the curse and point out the problem, they would immediately come under attack by the People of the Lie. Furthermore, the prison of power, pride, and prejudice was so impregnable that anyone who suggested the prisoner was in chains would be labeled as a madman, vilified, and condemned.

How could the People of the Lie be in chains? They are the good people! How could they be diseased? They are powerful, pure, rich, blessed, and, therefore, good. How could anyone suggest that they could be wrong in any way? They do not need liberation. They do not need healing. They do not need redemption. They are good. They are the best. They are right.

This is the world the Secret Son came into. This is the Sin of the World that confronted Him. Once we understand this dynamic, we can understand the battle in which He was engaged from the beginning. As soon as He appeared on the scene at His baptism, the enemy attacked. That's why, straightway after the baptism, He was thrown into the arena with Satan in the desert.

The Lord Jesus knew who the enemy was. It was not the prostitute or the thieving tax collector. It was not the heretic Samaritan. It was not the drunk or the addict. It was not the downtrodden, persecuted poor. It was not the blind, the lame, the lepers, or the diabolically possessed. It was not even the Roman overlords with their spears and swords.

The enemy was Satan and his children—the People of the Lie. Who did the Lord Jesus condemn? Who were the *only* ones He condemned? The People of the Lie. Who did He call sons of Satan? Who did He name as "whitewashed tombs," a "nest of vipers," and who did He say would rot forever in the steaming trash heap of Gehenna?

It was the respectable religious leaders: the scribes and masters of the law and the scholars of religion. It was the Pharisees with their self-righteous, do-gooder legalism. It was the Sadducees with their snobbish, wealthy, aristocratic ways. They were the enemy, not because of their education, their good works, or their wealth, but because they were the People of the Lie.

These, indeed, were the sons of Satan. They followed the ancient pattern of evil down to the last detail. They gathered together in an alliance against the Lord Jesus. This is what the People of the Lie always do; any enemy of their enemy is their friend. The scribes, Pharisees, Sadducees, followers of King Herod, and the Romans were mortal enemies most of the time, but Jesus Christ, the Secret Son, brought them together.

Once they gathered against Him, they did what the People of the Lie always do. Because they themselves could not possibly be the problem, they identified the one who *was* the problem—this country preacher from Galilee.

The Gospel writers lay out the terrifying story step by step. The conflict escalates according to the sinister pattern of the Sin of the World. First, they suspect Him. Then they question Him. Then they accuse Him. Then they gather the crowd against Him. Then they go for the final solution. The scapegoat must die. He must die painfully and publicly. There will be blood. There must be blood.

Howling for Revenge, the murderous mob follow through. The scapegoat is given a mock trial. The bloodthirsty crowd bays for His blood. He is beaten and hounded in the streets. Then the ritual sacrifice is made. The blood of the Lamb is poured out. The victim is hung on the tree for all to see. Satisfaction follows. The problem has been solved.

And this is how the Secret Son defeated the Sin of the World. He defeated it from the inside out. Because He was truly innocent, He was able to say to His accusers, "Do you want to blame someone? Blame me. You want to shift your own sin? Let me take it." Because He accepts death as the Lamb of God, He defeats the Dark Lord at his own grim game.

God Himself takes the blame. God Himself gathers up the Sin of the World and defeats it with an embrace.

This is the full, final sacrifice. This is the sacrifice on which all others fixed their eyes. Here the ransomed Isaac and the ram, the Passover lamb, the scapegoat, and all the bloody, mindless sacrifices of all the pagan religions everywhere in the world are both fulfilled and abolished forever.

Here the sacrifice that made peace between warring parties was fulfilled. Here the sacrifices for forgiveness were transcended. Here the sacrifices to seal a covenant between two tribes was realized. Here the scapegoat, onto whom the sins of the people were projected, was manifested.

This is what all the barbaric human sacrifices down the ages looked toward, and here they are obliterated forever because they are transcended. That which was a dark prediction of the future is vanquished by the fulfillment of the foreshadowing. Here all the sacrifices in all the cultures of the world are wiped away by the one, full, final sacrifice. They simply vanish and fade as the vampire beast shrivels and dies at the rising of the sun.

This is why the Lord Jesus came: to be the Lamb. This is why He came: to take the blame. This is why He came: to rescue Adam. This is why He came: to smash the Sin of the World once and for all, to vanquish the dark by the coming of His light.

He who became the victim also became the victor.

12

Victim and Victor

Situated on the southwestern side of Jerusalem is the Valley of Gehenna—the valley of death. In the days of the Old Testament, Gehenna held the cultic shrine of the gruesome god Moloch.

The image of Moloch was a huge, hollow, bronze statue. With the head of a bull and the body of a man, Moloch was an image of the minotaur. A fire burned within the base of the statue. The bull's mouth gaped wide, and his strong arms were outstretched to receive the offering. One by one, parents would bring their children and place them in the burning hands of the god, and the child would roll screaming through the mouth and down into the fiery furnace.

During the ceremony, the pagan priests beat drums and chanted to drown out the screams of the children and the disconsolate moans of the mothers.

Moloch the minotaur, the demon—half bull and half man— demanded innocent victims. Remember that this same minotaur lurks within the depths. We have encountered him before. Beneath Minos's palace he devoured young men and maidens. In the Valley of Gehenna and the city of Carthage and all around the ancient world, the servants of the Dark Lord demanded the blood of innocent victims.

Moloch is the god of this world. He is the demon who orchestrates the Sin of the World. He is the Minotaur, the Lord of the World, the Lord of the Flies, and the Father of Lies. This terrible image of Moloch can help us to understand in a new way what the full, final sacrifice of the Secret Son accomplished.

Jewish tradition held that the caves of Gehenna were the doorway to the underworld. Moloch is the lord of hell, and when the Hebrews finally banished him and his brother Baal, the Valley of Gehenna became an accursed place. Many believe that by the time of Jesus, Gehenna was used as a garbage dump and sewage pit. The bodies of executed criminals were thrown there. A fire burned continually. Scavenger dogs, vultures, and maggots infested the place. It stank of dead bodies, rank sewage, and decaying garbage. "Gehenna" became the word for hell. It was Moloch's palace.

The horrible, child-devouring statue of Moloch stands for the Dark Lord's reign of death over the whole world. Think of this stinking, fly-swarming, sewage-laden, blood-dripping hole as the throne room of Satan. This place, in all its horror, is a true image of the Sin of the World.

It is the mission of the Secret Son to penetrate this vile pit and shatter it from the inside out. How was He to do this? By becoming one of the victims Himself. When the People of the Lie captured Him, beat Him, rigged His trial, and had Him hauled off to death, the place of His execution and burial actually overlooked the Valley of Gehenna—Moloch's pit.

The People of the Lie took the Secret Son and fed Him into the mouth of Moloch. He slid into that hellish gullet, and the Dark Lord of death devoured Him just as surely as Moloch had devoured the innocent children of Israel so many centuries before.

But there was a trick in store that Satan could not have predicted. The Secret Son is the Son of God, and God is the source of all that is—He is Life itself. When Jesus Christ was devoured by Moloch, the Dark Lord unwittingly swallowed the Lord of Life and so consumed the seed of his own destruction.

The Lord of Death—the Great Moloch—collapsed from the inside out. The Death Star exploded. The dark tower of Mordor caved in on itself. The Lord of Death could not contain the Lord of Life any more than the darkness can hold back the dawn or the freezing cold extinguish the flame.

So, on the third day the Lord of Life burst forth from within the belly of Moloch, and Moloch was shattered from the inside out. The bonds of death were broken by Him who was bound. He became the Sin of the World, and so in dying, the Sin of the World died. The victim became the victor, and it was *only* by becoming the victim that He could become the victor.

This is why we cannot really speak about the Cross of Christ without also speaking of the empty tomb. His Cross and resurrection are two parts of the same mystery. He is victim and victor—victor because He was victim, and He became a victim in order to become a victor.

This is the answer to the question posed at the beginning of this book. This is the way Jesus Christ's death and resurrection "takes away the Sin of the World." This is how He "died to save us from our sins."

Through this action of the Secret Son, the Minotaur was eviscerated, Cerberus was beheaded, and the harpies went howling into the everlasting dark.

Don't be mistaken or mislead; this death was not simply the death of a martyr. It was not the tragic death of a man caught up in events that were over his head. This was not a political assassination or even simply the scapegoating of an innocent man by a rabid crowd.

All of that may have been true if Christ had not risen from the dead, but when He rose again, it suddenly became as clear and bright as a spring morning that something else of cosmic importance had taken place. The old dragon was slain. The Nazgûl was beheaded. The foul Balrog was thrown into the pit whence it came. The slaves were set free. Death was defeated. The Sin of the World was taken away — taken away forever.

The key battle had been won, but now the mopping-up operation needed to begin. The pattern was now established for the continuing war against the Dark Lord of this world. The pattern is simple to understand, but difficult to put into practice — as simple and as difficult as becoming a saint. The Little Lady and the Secret Son have shown the way for each of their followers to wage the war and win peace.

The first two words to remember are "small" and "secret." God began His infiltration of death's dark kingdom with a small secret. The Virgin Mary — the Little Lady — was small, and her Son was secret. The third word that completes this beautiful little trinity is "sacrifice."

The Secret Son and the Little Lady bring about the secret sacrifice. He said it Himself: "The Son of Man did not come to be served, but to serve and to give his life as a ransom for many."

God's way is always small, secret, and sacrificial. This is why the Cross of Christ is central to everything. Once we realize how the death and resurrection of Jesus Christ takes away the Sin of the World, the next thing we need to do is discover how to take up our crosses and follow Him. The astonishing words of St. Paul will echo in our hearts: "We preach Christ and Him crucified" and "I have resolved to know nothing but the Cross of Christ."

The first step on that way of the cross is the path of penitence. Only the penitent man may pass.

13

Only the Penitent Man May Pass

In the third Indiana Jones film, our hero is on a quest to find the Holy Grail—the chalice used by Our Lord at the Last Supper. At the climax of the film, the villain shoots and wounds Dr. Jones's father and snarls at Indy, "It's time to ask yourself what you believe, Dr. Jones." The Holy Grail has healing powers that would save the life of Indiana's father, but it is in a cave at the other end of a tunnel, and in order to reach it, one must pass three tests. Others have entered the tunnel and met a terrible fate—their heads sliced off by a spinning blade.

Indiana has the secret password for each of the three tests, so, to save his father's life, he plunges into the tunnel. As he does, he remembers the first password: "Only the penitent man may pass." Terrified by the swishing blade, he mutters, "Only the penitent man may pass. Only the penitent man may pass." Then it dawns on him to kneel in penitence, and as he does, the wicked blade whirls over him, and he rolls to safety.

While the Sin of the World is a cosmic, complex network of evil, it is also a multinational in which all of us have purchased shares. Power, pride, and prejudice dominate the structures of the world, but they also dominate our own lives. Resentment, Rivalry, and Revenge reign not only in the world, but also in our own hearts.

There is, however, an antidote to this poison. It is a small, secret, and sacrificial answer. It is called penitence—taking the blame, admitting we're guilty, and saying we're sorry.

Only the penitent man may pass.

Once you see the depth of the problem, the simplicity of the solution becomes obvious. Power, pride, and prejudice are rooted in the assumption that *I am right*. I must be right because I have chosen this particular path, and I would not have chosen it if it were not right. Because I am right, others must be wrong.

This is the insidious root of the Sin of the World, but it is countered by the simple genius of repentance. When we repent—when we truly and honestly repent—we are admitting, "Whoops. I got it wrong. In fact, I am *not* right. I messed up. I'm guilty. It's my fault." Even if it is partially someone else's fault, we're accepting our part of the blame and not shifting it to anyone else.

This simple admission hammers power on the head, since it is a laying down of power. It hammers pride on the head, since it is a humble admission that I am wrong. It hammers prejudice on the head, because if I am wrong, it could be that you are right after all.

Not only is repentance the simple answer to power, pride, and prejudice. It is also the answer to Resentment, Rivalry, and Revenge. Why? Because if I am guilty, if I am to blame, if my problems are my fault, then my Resentment dries up. When I take the blame, there is no one to feel resentful toward.

If I admit that the problem is my fault, then I take responsibility for myself, my thoughts, and my actions. If it is my fault, then Rivalry also evaporates, because I no longer need to view others as my deadly rivals. I can live and let live. When the rivals disappear, so does the need for Revenge. If, through repentance, I take the blame, I can let go of the relentless desire for Revenge.

Repentance, therefore, also pulls the plug on the scapegoat mechanism. If the problem is with me, I don't have to find another person, another tribe, another nation, or another race onto whom I can shift the blame. I can forget all that and take responsibility for solving the problem myself. I no longer need the scapegoat.

We are inclined to see repentance as simply going to Confession and telling the priest the grubby things we've done. But repentance is far greater than that. Repentance actually changes the world, and here's why: before the Lord Jesus defeated the Sin of the World, the entire human race was imprisoned by the demonic dynamic of power, pride, prejudice, Resentment, Rivalry, and Revenge. Not only were we trapped in this cycle of death, but we could see no way out. We could not break free, even if we knew we were in chains.

The Lord Jesus broke that spell by stepping up and taking the responsibility upon Himself. "You want to blame somebody? Blame me," He said. "I'll take the guilt. I'll pick up the trash. I'll take this sick cycle and break it from the inside out." When He did this, He opened the way for human beings to take responsibility for themselves. He gave us the power to make a truly free and independent choice to change the situation, change ourselves, and change the world.

We take freedom of choice for granted, but in the ancient world—and in every non-Christian society—people are fatalistic. In other words, they believe they have no choice and no power. They are at the mercy of the whims of the gods or that they are at the mercy of men far more powerful than they are. They do not have the power to change the world. All they can do is offer more and more sacrifices in a vain attempt to appease and please the gods.

But once the power of repentance is unlocked, human beings can take responsibility for their part in the Sin of the World. And as soon as they do, they become free to change and become agents of change in the world.

This is the paradox of power and pride: by laying down our pride through repentance, we actually gain genuine power because now we are taking responsibility for ourselves, and if for ourselves, then also for others. Once we understand this, we understand the mystery of forgiveness. Forgiveness is not merely letting someone off the hook. Forgiveness is not pretending that a grievance didn't really matter. Forgiveness is the other side of repentance. If repentance means taking responsibility for ourselves, then forgiveness means taking responsibility for another person's fault. As the Lord Jesus picked up our trash, forgiveness is picking up another person's trash.

When we forgive, we are repenting for another person, if you will. As Jesus stepped up and said, "I'll take the blame," so we say to the person who has offended us, "I'll take responsibility for that." It's over. The offense is obliterated with an embrace.

The next step in battling the darkness within is the step of faith. We speak about *the* Faith, referring to the Christian religion. Sometimes we speak of "having faith," as if we are trying very hard to believe something we know, deep down, isn't really true. Sometimes faith is equated with the intellectual assent to certain doctrinal statements. We have "faith" in the statements of the Creed, for example. Sometimes we speak of faith as trust in God, trust that He will provide for us and protect us.

Faith includes all these things, but at its heart, it is something more. Christian faith follows from repentance. Once we accept that we are to blame for our part in the Sin of the World, we also accept that, by our own power, we can do nothing about it. Sure, we might try very hard through self-discipline to battle against evil, but the odds are against us. The powers of darkness are greater than our weak efforts.

So we turn instead to the One who has already defeated these dark forces, and we sign up as members of His army. We turn to Jesus Christ, who broke the power of Satan, and we align ourselves with His victory. We look to Him not only as our example and guide, but also as the supernatural source of spiritual energy and strength.

We align ourselves with His victory by putting ourselves *into* Christ, His Cross, and His resurrection. This is what St. Paul means when he writes, "Are you unaware that we who were baptized into Christ Jesus were baptized into his death?" (Rom. 6:3). He repeats, we "were baptized into Christ" (Gal. 3:27). We have "put on the Lord Jesus Christ" (Rom. 13:14). Jesus Christ is "in us" (see 2 Cor. 13:5). This is not just a metaphor, a symbol, or a religious way of speaking.

It is a reality.

We really have been plunged into Christ and into the victory He won two thousand years ago.

Jesus taught the same lesson: we are to live "in Him and He in us." He is the vine, and we are the branches. If we remain in Him, we will bear much fruit, but without Him we can do nothing (see John 15:5). The power unleashed by the death of Christ lives in us. We have His Spirit within us so that we can "remain in Him and He in us" (1 John 4:13).

To live in this faith is to abide, day by day, in the victory of Christ over evil. But remembering that His victory is completely one with His being a victim, we also see that to live in Him is to live in the Lamb of God—and to live in the Lamb of God, we must walk in the Way of the Lamb.

The Way of the Lamb is the way of forgiveness—first for ourselves and then for others. This Way of the Lamb begins by apprehending the mystery of the Lamb and His mission—at the depth of our being—perhaps for the very first time.

14

Behold the Lamb

We live in Greenville, South Carolina — the buckle of the Bible Belt. Catholics here are in a minority. We're often challenged about our Faith by our fervent Baptist neighbors.

They might ask why we "worship Mary" or "pray to dead people" or why we call our priests "Father" when Jesus said, "Call no man Father." Another one of their favorites is, "Why do you Catholics have Jesus on the Cross in your churches? Don't you know He's risen from the dead?"

In answer, we say, "Don't y'all know your Bible? We have Jesus on the Cross because Paul says in 1 Corinthians 1:23, 'We preach Christ and Him crucified.'"

For St. Paul, the Cross was the center of history and the center of all human life. He understood that the sacrifice of the Lord Jesus was a mystical transaction of cosmic importance.

It was through this terrible mystery that the Sin of the World was conquered. It was through this death that the hidden foundations of all the violence and hatred in the world crumbled.

Therefore, St. Paul makes it clear that the central image of the Christian Faith is the crucified man. The horror of the naked man nailed to the tree has caused many to turn away in disgust, confusion, and fear. How bizarre and scandalous that the central image of a great religion should be the corpse of an executed criminal! But St. Paul understood the horror of the Cross: "The message of the Cross is foolishness to those who are perishing, but to us who are being saved it is the power of God.... But we proclaim Christ crucified, a stumbling block to Jews and foolishness to Gentiles" (1 Cor. 1:18–23).

The Cross and resurrection are the good news. This action is *the* event. Without it, Christianity is nothing but a collection of sweet sayings and good works, but through it, we are in Christ and Christ is in us — through it, we are given the hope of glory.

Therefore, we do not apologize. With St. Paul, we preach Christ crucified. We have no other gospel.

To truly grasp this reality, we must "behold the Lamb." From the beginning of the Gospel, John the Baptist cries out, "Behold the Lamb!" The Lamb of God crucified is the center of our Faith. This is why the General Instruction of the Roman Missal states, "Either on the altar or near it, there is to be a cross, with the figure of Christ crucified upon it, a cross clearly visible to the assembled people."

It is "the old, rugged Cross, the emblem of suffering and shame." When we see the crucifix, our heart should sing, "In the Cross of Christ I glory, towering o'er the wrecks of time."

Because the crucifixion of the Lord Jesus demolishes the Sin of the World from the inside out, the Church keeps the image of that profound and astounding victory as her central focus.

We not only preach Christ crucified, but we understand that this critical, cosmic crucifixion is not simply a past historical event. Jesus said with His dying breath, "It is accomplished." "Mission accomplished" was not, however, the end of the story, but the beginning.

The mission was to break open the prison and set the captives free. The death and resurrection of Christ began a chain reaction that would eventually liberate the whole human race and the entire planet. To understand what this means, we have to examine the meaning of what I have called a "mystical transaction on a cosmic level."

When the Lord Jesus died, a new power was unleashed into the world that the world had never seen and which the Lord of this World — the Prince of Darkness — could never have imagined. The torture, death, and resurrection of the Lord Jesus broke open the floodgates of a new power of life and love in the world. This new power of abundant life could not have been broken open in any other way. The new power being poured out is symbolized by the blood and water that gushed from the Lord Jesus' side when it was pierced by the centurion's spear.

Think of a dam breaking. Think of lightning flashing across the night sky. Think of a trumpet blast, a burst of nuclear power, or an explosion. The power released by the death of the Lord Jesus was a spiritual bomb blast. This burst of spiritual power took place because the Lord of Life Himself was broken open.

Think of the Lord Jesus as a clay vessel filled with the universal power and life of God Himself. When that clay vessel of His body was broken, the power of the Creator, the power of the one who is the Foundation and Source of All Existence burst into the unsuspecting world. It exploded right in the middle of death's dream kingdom.

No wonder the Father of Lies howled in frustrated rage and arrogant fury!

The Way of the Lamb is first to be plunged into the death of Christ and then to come up gasping with life, like a newborn baby or a drowning man just breaking the water's surface. Then one must continue to live out the Way of the Lamb by giving our lives as a secret and small sacrifice.

As St. Paul teaches, "I urge you brothers ... to offer your bodies as a living sacrifice, holy and pleasing to God, your spiritual worship" (Rom. 12:1). As we do this, we participate in and perpetuate Christ's sacrificial victory in the world today.

I should further stress that this is not merely the religious routine of saying our prayers and being committed to the corporal works of mercy. Yes, we feed the poor. We educate the young. We house the homeless. We heal the sick. We liberate the prisoners. We fight for peace. We battle against the culture of death. We counsel the lonely and bury the dead. We do all these things and more, but we do them in the first place because we have identified with the Crucified One. We can do all things through Christ who strengthens us (see Phil. 4:13).

If we have not had this foundational transformation, then all our good works are merely good works. They have value, yes, but they are not a participation in the mystical, cosmic victory over the Sin of the World, which was won by the Lord Jesus Christ—victim and victor. But if we are living in the Way of the Lamb, every prayer and good action becomes part of His victory over evil.

The explosion of life and love into the world that came about through the death and resurrection of the Lord Jesus, and is continued through the life of the Church, is hinted at in a mysterious passage from St. Paul's letter to the Colossians. He says about the Cross, "I have become its servant by the commission God gave me to present to you ... the mystery that has been kept hidden for ages and generations, but is now disclosed to the Lord's people. To them God has chosen to make known among the Gentiles the glorious riches of this mystery, which is Christ in you, the hope of glory" (see Col. 1:24–27).

Paul says that this mystery has been hidden for ages and generations. What mystery is this? It is the mystery of the Sin of the World and its sudden and unimaginable solution. What else does Christ's death and resurrection accomplish? "Christ in you. The hope of glory." Paul continues, "He is the one we proclaim, admonishing and teaching everyone with all wisdom, so that we may present everyone fully mature in Christ. To this end I strenuously contend with all the energy Christ so powerfully works in me."

The explosion of life and love implants Christ-life into us so that we might become all that God created us to be.

The Way of the Lamb is, therefore, a path to a fullness of life that we cannot attain simply through good works, self-discipline, and self-help. It means living in a new dimension of reality—a supernatural renewal of heart and mind that draws us ever closer into an intimate union with the Lord Jesus Himself.

If you have never understood this truth before, it is not enough simply to understand it with your head. It is a reality to be embraced. The Way of the Lamb is a personal choice.

You can stop reading this book right now and take a step that will change your life. You can simply and honestly behold the Lamb, perhaps for the first time. To behold the Lamb means to gaze on the Cross of Christ and say from the bottom of your being, "Lord Jesus Christ, Son of the Living God, Living Lamb of God, have mercy on me, a sinner! Here I am, standing before You. Just as I am, without one plea, O Lamb of God, I come."

This first step in the Way of the Lamb is absolutely vital, and if you have already taken that step, do it again. Do it now. Do it every day of your life, for in this way you will walk in the Way of the Lamb and live your life in a new dimension of reality.

That this life on a supernatural level is possible is revealed to us by the saints. The saints are ordinary people who have become extraordinary through union with the Crucified and Risen One.

As St. Paul said, "They know nothing but the love of Christ and Him crucified. For them to live *is* Christ." The saints are unique, living icons of the Crucified and Risen Master. Each of the saints in his or her own way reveals the Crucified and Risen to the world.

Each of the saints unlocks that powerhouse of love and life in the world. Each of the saints sets off an explosion of the life of the Lord Jesus in the middle of death's dark kingdom.

The Way of the Lamb continues to release this death-defying power into the world, most potently through the gift of martyrdom. Have you ever wondered why the Church honors martyrs so much? It is not only because they have shown heroic virtue. It is not only because they have exhibited superhuman courage. It is not only because they have been faithful witnesses to the love of Christ.

There is more to it than that, and the explanation lies in one of the most mysterious verses of the Bible. In his letter to the Colossians, St. Paul writes, "Now I rejoice in what I am suffering for you, and I fill up in my flesh what is still lacking in regard to Christ's afflictions, for the sake of His body, which is the Church." The apostle says that his own physical suffering is a share in Christ's suffering and that it fills what is still lacking in Christ's afflictions.

What could this mean? Christ's death was the full, final sacrifice. We say it was "once and for all," and by that we usually mean "one and done." But could it, in fact, mean "once and for all time and continuing in all time?" The death of Christ was a cosmic event, and, therefore, it transcended time and space. It was real on that afternoon outside Jerusalem two thousand years ago, but it was also real in the hints and guesses of the Old Testament and in a thousand other religions around the world.

It was "then", but it is also "now," and that astounding mystery lives in all time and lives today in the lives of the saints.

The martyrs are honored because, in the shedding of their blood, they complete what is lacking in the Cross of Christ. The shedding of the blood of the martyrs continues to break open that flood of grace and power in the world. Each time a martyr's life is taken, each time their blood is shed, the sacrifice of Christ is renewed in the cosmos, the life-giving power of the Crucified and Risen One bursts through once again.

When we come to realize the depth and power of this truth, we also come to realize that this is the primary mission of the Church. This is why the Church is here, and this is why we are here—not just to be missionaries or social workers. We are not here simply to make the world a better place. We are not here only to do good. We are here to walk in the Way of the Lamb. We are here to offer our participation in that one full, final sacrifice. Every action of self-sacrifice—no matter how secret and small—helps to bring alive in every moment and hammer home the eternal victory of the Crucified. We are here as witnesses to that action, and the word "witness" means "martyr."

The people of the ancient world practiced their sacrifices in the vain attempts to appease their cruel and heartless gods. They focused their fears and rage on their helpless victims and believed the sacrifices somehow brought peace and reconciliation. And they were not so far off.

All their sacrifices pointed to that one full, final sacrifice. The children, the bulls, goats, and lambs they offered all pointed to the one Lamb—the Lamb of God—whose death and resurrection fulfilled all their empty rituals and nullified the need for them forever.

That one full, final sacrifice continues to be alive and applied in our lives every day as each one of the baptized follows in the

Way of the Lamb—the way of mystical union with the Crucified and Risen One.

These daily offerings are confirmed and magnified by that other daily offering of the whole Church—the sacrifice of the altar in the mystery of the Mass.

15

Liturgy and Liberty

If you want to understand the grim reality of ritual sacrifice, look no further than Mel Gibson's astonishing film *Apocalypto*. It is set in the disintegrating Mayan culture of the sixteenth century. The Mayan warriors capture whole neighboring tribes and march them to their city in the jungle where the victims are hauled, one by one, to the top of a pyramid to be gutted and beheaded.

The demonic dynamic of power, pride, and prejudice, which culminates first in blame and then in the ritual slaughter of others, is played out in all its gruesome gore in Gibson's film. The Mayans and Aztecs were especially bloodthirsty, but the same murderous offering of the scapegoat echoes like horrifying screams through the annals of antiquity. When they weren't sacrificing humans, the ancients substituted animals. Grain, oil, and wine could also be offered to the gods, but blood was always required for the most effective sacrifice.

Once the "blameworthy" people were killed, it seemed the tribe's problems were solved. The blood that was shed would bring peace to the troubled people. The gods would be happy. They would bless the tribe with prosperity and power. The ancient peoples understood that the dark ritual killing somehow penetrated down into the deepest part of their humanity. They felt that the demons, howling and growling within the subterranean labyrinth of their own hearts, would be quieted, appeased, and purged.

But we don't do that anymore, right? We've grown out of it. We're modern people. We don't appease monster, demon gods with blood sacrifices. We don't cut the throats of chickens and splatter their blood on a voodoo doll. Religion isn't about that, is it? We now know that religion is about being nice people, working for justice, and making the world a better place.

We're not superstitious. We don't need to do that sacrifice thing anymore, right? Jesus Himself said, "Go and learn the meaning of the words, 'I desire mercy, not sacrifice'" (Matt. 9:13). The Book of Hebrews says that daily sacrifice isn't necessary anymore. Jesus paid the price. His sacrifice ends sacrifice, doesn't it?

Modern man believes he has progressed in this way, that he has moved on from those primitive religions devoted to strange gods. Has it ever occurred to you, then, how strange it is that there is one religion in the modern world that still practices sacrifice? Not only is it the only major religion that does so, but it is the world's largest single religion.

Catholics claim that a sacrifice is offered whenever Mass is celebrated.

Listen closely to the language of the Mass. The priest talks about offering the sacrifice all throughout the liturgy. He says, "Pray, brothers and sisters, that my sacrifice and yours may be acceptable to God the Almighty Father." The people reply, "May the Lord accept the sacrifice at your hands ..." The priest continues to pray that God accept "these gifts, these offerings, these holy and unblemished sacrifices." He also refers to "this victim, this pure victim, this spotless victim."

The whole ritual is awash in the language of sacrifice.

Is this just a historic curiosity? Is it a relic of a more primitive time when people still thought sacrifice was necessary? Certainly for the last five hundred years, there have been massive efforts to weed out the sacrificial language from the Mass; the Protestant reformers denied that the Mass was a sacrifice, and Catholic modernists have shifted the emphasis away from the idea of sacrifice, downgrading the Mass to no more than a family meal at a table.

As a priest, I resist this heresy with all my heart. The Mass is a sacrifice, and it is more vital now than ever to insist that it is a sacrifice.

What kind of sacrifice is it? The *Catechism of the Catholic Church* teaches:

> The Eucharist is thus a sacrifice because it re-presents (makes present) the sacrifice of the Cross, because it is its memorial and because it applies its fruit:
>
> > [Christ], our Lord and God, was once and for all to offer Himself to God the Father by His death on the altar of the Cross, to accomplish there an everlasting redemption. But because His priesthood was not to end with His death, at the Last Supper "on the night when he was betrayed," [He wanted] to leave to His beloved spouse, the Church, a visible sacrifice (as the nature of man demands) by which the bloody sacrifice, which He was to accomplish once for all on the Cross, would be re-presented, its memory perpetuated until the end of the world, and its salutary power be applied to the forgiveness of the sins we daily commit.

The *Catechism* continues:

> The sacrifice of Christ and the sacrifice of the Eucharist
> are one single sacrifice: The victim is one and the same:
> the same now offers through the ministry of priests, who
> then offered himself on the cross; only the manner of
> offering is different.
>
> And since in this divine sacrifice, which is celebrated
> in the Mass, the same Christ who offered Himself once
> in a bloody manner on the altar of the Cross is contained
> and is offered in an un-bloody manner.... This sacrifice
> is truly propitiatory.
>
> The Eucharist is also the sacrifice of the Church. The
> Church, which is the body of Christ, participates in the of-
> fering of her Head. With Him, she herself is offered whole
> and entire. She unites herself to His intercession with the
> Father for all men. In the Eucharist, the sacrifice of Christ
> becomes also the sacrifice of the members of His body.
> The lives of the faithful, their praise, sufferings, prayer,
> and work are united with those of Christ and with His
> total offering, and so acquire a new value. Christ's sacrifice
> present on the altar makes it possible for all generations
> of Christians to be united with His offering (1367–1368).

Through the sacrifice of the Mass, we are united with the
timeless, once and for all sacrifice of the Lord Jesus. This is not
just a symbol or nice religious language. It is a reality, a mystical
union, a contract and covenant through which we identify and
become one with the action that broke the power of Satan and
shattered forever the Sin of the World.

Why is it important to insist that the Mass is a sacrifice?
Because the crucifixion of Jesus Christ was a sacrifice. It was not

just a tragic martyrdom. The Mass is the way we bring into the present moment and participate fully in the event that changed the world and rescued the human race forever.

The sacrifice of the Mass, therefore, keeps alive and applies the power of that cosmic event. Every time the sacrifice of the Mass is celebrated, the sacrifice of Jesus Christ—victim and victor—is made alive and present. Every time the sacrifice of the Mass is celebrated, Satan's ultimate destiny of defeat is furthered.

But there is more. You will remember from the first part of this book that the Sin of the World is hidden. Power, pride, and prejudice are concealed beneath our glittering facades. We are blind to the Resentment, Rivalry, and Revenge that seethe in our hearts. These dark urges surge beneath the surface. The monsters lurk in the labyrinth of our memories, hearts, and minds.

The Sin of the World is deeper than words. It lies like a serpent in a cavern below our conscious minds. It writhes deep within the sub-linguistic realm of our being. It is way down deep in the dungeon of our souls. This is the dark place where the wild things are. This is the prison house where we are chained. And this is the place that most needs the healing light of Christ. But how do we get down to that dark place?

Psychologists say we can access these depths of the personality through various techniques. We may go into the depths during our dreams, through specialized counseling, hypnosis, or even mind-bending drugs. Spiritual masters know that we also have access to the deepest areas of our hearts through meditation and repetitious prayer but also through ceremonious ritual.

This is an awesome and amazing truth: it is through ritualistic words and actions that we open the cellar door. It is through the language of symbol and sign that we enter the realm below language. It is through repeated ritual and ceremony that we engage with the emotions and instincts that lie below our conscious descriptions and explanations.

This is why the sacraments are referred to as mysteries because a mystery is something that can be experienced, even though it cannot be explained. Through the sacraments—the Sacred Mysteries—the mystery of the Lord Jesus' death and resurrection is experienced, even though it cannot be explained.

We participate in the Mass not simply by saying the prayers, singing the hymns, and listening to the homily. Instead, through the Mass, as in Baptism, we are plunged into the death and resurrection of Christ, and this participation happens at the deepest level of our being.

This is the real reason the Mass should be celebrated in a traditional, formal, ceremonial, and ritualistic way. It is not celebrated this way just because "Father likes all that fancy, traditional stuff." A ceremonial celebration of the Mass is not simply a matter of taste. When the clergy are robed, when the altar servers move in a formal pattern, when the words, music, and gestures of the celebration are ritualistic, we respond in the depths of our being. The beauty of architecture, music, vestments, incense, and gesture speak to us in a language beyond words—the language of beauty. This supernal language reaches down to the depths of our souls, the place deeper than words where the Sin of the World is most deeply lodged.

This is why the modernist celebration of the Mass is a travesty. Not simply because the buildings are brutal and the music banal. It is not only because the Mass has been turned into a sentimental family celebration with shallow prayers and bland politically correct preaching. The modernist celebration of the Mass is appalling not merely because these things are an error in taste, but because the real power of the sacrifice of the Mass is being emasculated. The depth of experience that takes place through ceremony and ritual is being watered down. The Cross of our Lord Jesus Christ is being minimized and its true power over evil negated.

The Cross of Jesus Christ towers over the wrecks of time. It reaches into the greatest depths and raises humanity to the highest glories. The Cross broke humanity's addiction to power, pride, and prejudice. It answered Resentment, Rivalry, and Revenge, and it is through the sacrifice of the Mass that this once for all sacrifice is made real within the depths of our humanity. It is there, day by day in a thousand churches and chapels, that the cosmic Cross of Christ, which defeated the demons, is brought into the present moment and applied for our needs and the needs of the whole world.

Through the Mass, the victory of the Crucified has been celebrated on the field of battle and at the bedsides of dying kings. Through the Mass, the victory of the Crucified has been brought to poor orphans and starving prisoners in concentration camps and applied for the healing of lepers, the weeping reconciliation of bitter enemies, and the comfort of a dying martyr. It has brought the Crucified to bless the union of a hopeful bride and groom, the birth of a child, and the memory of the faithful departed.

The sacrifice of the Mass is nonnegotiable. Through this ancient ritual, this fragile, broken world still holds together. Through this sacrifice, the demons still flee, and nature groans for redemption. Without this sacrifice, the darkness would descend. The gates of hell would prevail. The center would not hold. All would slip away, and the demons would swarm like locusts to devour the world.

When we truly participate in the Mass at the deepest level of our being, we are plunged into that saving action. When we participate in the Mass, we are in Christ and Christ is in us. When we celebrate the Mass, we are preaching Christ crucified, risen, ascended, and glorified. When we celebrate Mass, we behold the Lamb of God, and we walk in the Way of the Lamb. When we celebrate Mass, we participate in and perpetuate Christ's one full, final sacrifice that takes away the Sin of the World.

When we celebrate Mass, we are joined with Jesus Christ, victim and victor, and this union provides the dynamic power of grace to walk in the way of the Christian warrior.

16

The Swords of the Spirit

Now let us get straight to the point, and the point is the point of a sword. The Christian life is a battle, or it is nothing at all. The baptized are warriors, and the Church is not mild; it is militant.

This entire book has been an attempt to hammer home the fact that the Lord Jesus came into this world to do battle with the ancient foe and that He won the victory with a stunning reversal. He was devoured by the Sin of the World and demolished it by bursting it from the inside out.

Therefore, St. Paul proclaims with triumph, "We preach Christ crucified," and he declares, "I resolved to know nothing … except Jesus Christ, and him crucified (1 Cor. 2:2). To engage in the battle is to be unified with the Crucified. It means saying with St. Paul, "For to me life is Christ, and death is gain" (Phil. 1:21) and "I have been crucified with Christ; yet I live, no longer I, but Christ lives in me; insofar as I now live in the flesh, I live by faith in the Son of God who has loved me and given himself up for me" (Gal. 2:19–20). We are identified with the Crucified. We live in Him and He in us. What remains for each one of us, then, is to walk in the Way of the Lamb and replicate the victory of the Lord Jesus in the world.

Thérèse of Lisieux is one of my favorite warrior saints. She wrote, "Sanctity! It must be won at the point of a sword!" She cried on her deathbed, "I will die with my weapons in my hand!" In that same spirit, this chapter gathers together ten foundation principles for the Christian warrior. I call them the Swords of the Spirit. The ten swords are ten words beginning with "s."

The first sword is the word "sacraments." Each one of the sacraments is a participation in the Cross and resurrection of Christ. We are buried with Him in Baptism and rise with Him into new life. At Confirmation, the covenant of the Cross is sealed. With the Eucharist, the victory of the Cross is brought into the present moment, and we share in the Body and Blood of Christ.

In marriage, we enter a nuptial unity with our spouse and with Christ. In ordination, the priest and deacon are uniquely configured to the Crucified. Through these sacraments, we enter into a covenant of sacrificial service to our spouse, our family, and the Church—the Bride of Christ.

In Confession and Anointing of the Sick, the sick and the sin-sick are healed by the blood and water from the side of the Crucified. The Seven Sacraments are the first Sword of the Spirit through which we are unified with the Crucified and live out His life in the world.

The second sword is Sacred Scripture. The Letter to the Hebrews proclaims, "The word of God is living and effective, sharper than any two-edged sword, penetrating even between soul and spirit, joints and marrow, and able to discern reflections and thoughts of the heart" (4:12). Scripture is a dynamic force in the battle. Inspired by the Holy Spirit in its composition, it is continually inspired through the interpretation of the Church and through the action of the Holy Spirit in our lives.

Pick up the sword of Scripture. Read a chapter of the Bible every day. Learn about the ancient practice of *Lectio Divina*, in which the monks teach us to meditate and so immerse our souls in the beauty and wisdom of the Scriptures. Memorize Scripture as you memorize your prayers, for the words of Sacred Scripture are powerful weapons in the spiritual battle.

The third virtue we learned from the Blessed Virgin. It is the word "small." How wonderful to remember that "small is beautiful." God chose the Little Lady to begin His work, and every work of His in the world starts small. The Lord Jesus taught this Himself when He said His kingdom was like a mustard seed — the smallest of seeds, which when planted, grows into a great tree.

If any human work or apostolate for God is great, be assured that it began small. God doesn't work any other way. Therefore, if we wish to replicate the victory of Christ, our work must be small. If it is small it will be authentic. If it is small it will be intimate. If it is small it will be real. If it is small it will be human-sized. If it is small it will be humble. If it is small it will be powerful.

The Lord Jesus told us we cannot enter the kingdom unless we become like little children. He did *not* say that was one option. He said it was the *only* option. Therefore, the third sword is the word "small," and the way to be small and remain small is by developing your devotion to the Little Lady.

Love Mary. Pray the Rosary. Make your dedication to the Immaculate Heart of Mary. Keep her image before you, and let the Little Lady of Nazareth be by your side. Let her words echo in your heart: "The Almighty has done great things for me, and holy is His name."

The fourth of the Swords of the Spirit is "secret." Remember the Secret Son. God's work in the world continues to be secret. Even when a church or ministry or apostolate has a public face, a public relations expert, or a media presence, if it is a Spirit-filled ministry, then behind the scenes there is a secret reality, and that is where the real action takes place. Ven. Archbishop Sheen had a national television presence. His words and works were known by millions, but his real life was his secret life of prayer. His daily holy hour was a top priority.

This secret life is the true life of the Christian warrior. It is there, in secret, that we draw closer to the Lord Jesus. It is in contemplation and the mystery of the Mass that we come to identify with the Crucified and so become living conduits of Christ's victory in the world.

The sword named "secret" is a reminder that exterior appearances are an illusion. The real work of God in our own lives and in the world is invisible. The secret history of the world is the one never recorded in the history books or trumpeted in the headlines. God's real work is always behind the scenes within the hearts of men and women, and it is always invisible.

This is because even now Satan, that proud spirit, still loves the limelight. He likes to strut and preen. He is a show-off, a braggart, an arrogant, vain, and posturing prince. He doesn't do "secret," but God does. And His true servants do, and it is through the secret agency of Divine Providence that the victory is still being won.

Therefore, if you would be a soldier in this army, you will be a member of the Lord's secret service. Your main work will be undercover, camouflaged by humility, and your unseen work will be one of your most powerful secret weapons.

The fifth Sword of the Spirit is the word "sacrifice." The main part of this book explains in detail the dynamic of sacrifice and how, through sacrifice, the victory over sin was won. But there is another more practical dimension to the principle of sacrifice.

It is this: just as Satan cannot understand the power of being small, so he can never understand self-sacrifice. As a fallen angel, Satan made his choice for pride and self-aggrandizement. His decision was complete and final. He wanted to be like God, and that is the definition of pride. For all eternity, this is his decision. He cannot, therefore, conceive of anything other than pride. He may look on self-sacrifice and wonder at it, but he can never admire it or understand it. As a deaf man cannot hear music, and a blind man cannot perceive color, the old dragon cannot comprehend self-sacrifice.

Therefore, every action of self-sacrifice, no matter how small, is a sword thrust into Satan's heart. This is the underlying principle, for example, of fasting and all forms of asceticism. This is the underlying principle of the corporal and spiritual works of mercy. This is the underlying strength of tithing our money self-sacrificially. We do not do these things simply because the hungry need to be fed and the homeless housed or because the parish priest needs to pay his bills. When we live out the Faith in a practical, sacrificial way we are living out the victory of the Cross, and each action of self-sacrifice, no matter how small, is one more stroke of the sword of sacrifice in the everlasting battle.

The sixth sword is the word "simplicity." Simplicity is powerful because it is a form of honesty. There are three aspects to the sword of simplicity. The first is simplicity of speech. It is a good and worthy thing to make a simple, solemn promise to never lie. Think about how often we lie to ourselves to excuse ourselves and how often we lie to others to please them or win their approval. Think of all the little lies just to get ourselves out of a scrape or to make life easier.

Simplicity of speech allows no lies—not even white lies to be polite and spare someone's feelings. Diplomacy and tact, kindness and sensitivity are required if we are to be simple in speech without being hurtful. Read the Gospels again, and study the simplicity of Jesus. He never lied. Not once.

Simplicity of speech brings about simplicity of life. The way to achieve simplicity of life is not to go on some sort of poverty campaign in which you secretly believe wealth and possessions are evil and that you are, therefore, superior because you are poor. No. This is not simplicity of life; it is another form of lying. Simplicity of life is the art of loving all things according to their worth.

Let us say you have a nice, expensive car. There is no sin in an expensive car, but why do you have that expensive car? Is it because it is a status symbol? That is not simplicity. Is it because you feel big and powerful because you can afford an expensive car? That is not simple. Is it because you can be better than others in your expensive car? That is not simple.

However, if you have a car that happens to be expensive because you have worked hard and can afford it, and you appreciate the car because it provides good, safe, reliable, and pleasant transportation for you and your family, then you are loving that thing according to its worth. That is what a car is for, and, in this way, you can own that car and still achieve simplicity. This principle applies to all our money and possessions. If we love them according to their worth we will be suitably detached from them.

If you want to know if you *are* detached and loving all things according to their worth, ask yourself if you would give that thing away. If you can, you are detached from it.

Simplicity of life leads to simplicity of person. If we vow never to lie and strive to live simply, then we will eventually come down to the place we ought to be. Pride will begin to evaporate, and we will become simple in the acceptance of who we truly are. The saint is not an extraordinary person, but an ordinary person who has become all that God created them to be. St. Francis de Sales said, "Be who you are, and be that well."

The seventh sword is "steadfast." The battle cannot be won unless we are focused for the long run. The way of the Christian Warrior is a marathon, not a dash. When faced with faults or sins in our lives we should not attempt to break them quickly, but to bend them slowly over time.

Nothing great was ever accomplished quickly. God plays a long game, and it's not over until the final trumpet. The ways of Providence are long and the journey complex. God is always working within us to bring about His will in His way, and most often, the greatest work He is doing is invisible to us. He works in secret, remember?

Therefore, what is required of us is patience, hard work, and the ability to never give up. Ever. We may stumble and fall into sin. But we get up. We may be discouraged and fall by the wayside because of the corruption of the Church and the hypocrisy of priests. But we get up and keep going. We may be troubled by tragedy, disappointed in others and ourselves, besieged by sickness, or devastated by the death of a loved one. But we get up. We do not stop. God is working His purpose out, and this is what faith is all about.

Being steadfast in the midst of hardship, disappointment, and failure is the mark of a saint. This is the sign of what the Church calls "heroic virtue." The saint never gives up. Even if he or she is plodding along, head down through the darkest tunnel with no sign of the light, the saint keeps going.

The eighth Sword of the Spirit is "silence." In the battle, there comes a time when speaking has ended. It has ended not because speech is useless, but because no one is listening, and they are not listening because they cannot listen. Sin has hardened their hearts.

There are three reasons silence is required. The first is the fact that, when discussion has become unreasonable, silence is the only resort. Speech is, by its very nature, rational. Words mean something. Grammar is the logical arrangement of words. Behind all language is rational thought and reasonable concepts, but if, because of relativism, reason is no longer functioning, then speech becomes pointless. The sign that silence is required is when discussion and debate dissolve into nothing but irrational emotion, sentimentality, and rage.

The second sign that silence is required is when speech is being used only to lie and obscure the truth. Satan and his children do not use language to discover and discuss the truth. They do not debate to reveal the truth. They use discussion and debate to avoid and twist the truth. They use argument to bully and manipulate people. They use language not as a tool of truth, but as a weapon of lies. When you observe that happening, silence becomes your weapon.

Finally, the third reason silence is required is the need for contemplative prayer. Silence can be the response to empty, lying words, but it can also be the response of the soul when it becomes clear that prayer has moved beyond language to the realm where communication is wordless, because it is above and beyond words. This silence is not only a refuge from lies; it is an immersion in truth. It is abiding in the truth of Jesus Christ who went to the Cross mute as a lamb to the slaughter. In silence we enter into the battle beyond words in a way beyond words.

Which brings me to the ninth Sword of the Spirit. It is the word "supernatural." The battle is in the supernatural realm, and it is fought with the supernatural gifts of grace. The supernatural sword is important for three reasons.

The first is that, when we remember that the battle is supernatural, we are reminded that "our struggle is not with flesh and blood but with the principalities, with the powers, with the world rulers of this present darkness, with the evil spirits in the heavens" (Eph. 6:12). We must keep this reality fresh in our minds. We are not just involved in the dull routine of good works, but we are engaged in the great cosmic battle.

The second reason the supernatural sword is important is that through this realization we are reminded that, if the battle is of cosmic importance, it is, therefore, of eternal significance. We are accomplishing things in the eternal realm, and it is in the eternal dimension that we will one day receive the reward.

The third reason the supernatural is vital to remember is that we can do nothing by our own strength. It is only through the supernatural gift of grace that we can do battle, and if we forget the supernatural dimension, we will soon lapse back into trying to walk in the way of the Christian warrior by our own strength—and that way leads to disaster.

The tenth and final Sword of the Spirit is "suffering." Sooner or later, in one way or another, each one of us will face suffering. It may come through a final sickness, it may come through a broken marriage, a broken family, or a broken heart. It may come through poverty, pain, or powerlessness. It may come through accident, tragedy, or trials unimaginable. But sooner or later, we will all face it.

As we face the terrible conundrum of suffering we also hold in our hands the crucifix—which is the answer. The answer is not an easy theological answer or a sentimental cliché. Instead, the answer is in the experience itself. Within the midst of the suffering we still cling to the old, rugged Cross. In the midst of the suffering, we are identified with the Crucified. It is in suffering that we are most fully unified with the Crucified.

It is in suffering that we join ourselves with the full, final sacrifice and, with St. Paul, make up what is lacking for the sake of the Church and for the redemption of the whole world. We wield these Swords of the Spirit knowing that, as we do, we are sharing in Christ's Cross so that we might also share in His eternal glory.

If we walk in the Way of the Lamb — the way of the Christian warrior — we will experience, at the very depth of our being, the transformation that is promised. Then we will have answered the question posed at the beginning of this book: "What on earth does it mean that Jesus died to take away the Sin of the World?"

We will not only know the answer with our head, but with our heart — and not only with our heart, but with every fiber of our being. At that point, we will sing with St. Paul, "I am resolved to know nothing but Christ and Him crucified" and "I have been crucified with Christ, and I no longer live, but Christ lives in me. The life I now live in the body, I live by faith in the Son of God, who loved me and gave Himself for me."

About the Author

A former Evangelical, Fr. Dwight Longenecker studied at Oxford and served as a priest in the Church of England before he and his family were received into the Catholic Church. He is the author of over twenty books and booklets on Catholic faith and culture as well as thousands of articles for various magazines, journals, and websites. He is a popular conference speaker, podcaster, and blogger. Follow his blog, browse his books, and be in touch at dwightlongenecker.com.

Sophia Institute

Sophia Institute is a nonprofit institution that seeks to nurture the spiritual, moral, and cultural life of souls and to spread the Gospel of Christ in conformity with the authentic teachings of the Roman Catholic Church.

Sophia Institute Press fulfills this mission by offering translations, reprints, and new publications that afford readers a rich source of the enduring wisdom of mankind.

Sophia Institute also operates the popular online resource CatholicExchange.com. *Catholic Exchange* provides world news from a Catholic perspective as well as daily devotionals and articles that will help readers to grow in holiness and live a life consistent with the teachings of the Church.

In 2013, Sophia Institute launched Sophia Institute for Teachers to renew and rebuild Catholic culture through service to Catholic education. With the goal of nurturing the spiritual, moral, and cultural life of souls, and an abiding respect for the role and work of teachers, we strive to provide materials and programs that are at once enlightening to the mind and ennobling to the heart; faithful and complete, as well as useful and practical.

Sophia Institute gratefully recognizes the Solidarity Association for preserving and encouraging the growth of our apostolate over the course of many years. Without their generous and timely support, this book would not be in your hands.

www.SophiaInstitute.com
www.CatholicExchange.com
www.SophiaInstituteforTeachers.org

Sophia Institute Press® is a registered trademark of Sophia Institute. Sophia Institute is a tax-exempt institution as defined by the Internal Revenue Code, Section 501(c)(3). Tax ID 22-2548708.